KEEP the BEAT

HEART HEALTHY RECIPES
from the National Heart, Lung, and Blood Institute

U.S. DEPARTMENT OF HEALTH AND HUMAN SERVICES
National institutes of Health
National Heart, Lung, and Blood Institute

TABLE OF CONTENTS

RECIPES

APPETIZERS AND SOUPS

MAIN DISHES

BEEF

PORK, LAMB, AND VEAL

CHICKEN

TURKEY

FISH

SIDE DISHES

BREADS

DESSERTS

TOPPINGS and SALAD DRESSINGS

BEVERAGES

HERE'S SOME TERRIFIC NEWS!

What's good for your heart is great for your taste buds.
As the recipes in this special collection will show,
you don't have to lose flavor to gain health.

Cooking up heart health requires no secret ingredients.
It simply means making dishes that are lower in saturated fat,
cholesterol, and total fat, and reduced in sodium. And, as an extra
plus, these dishes have fewer calories than those higher in fat. It
means enjoying "Crispy Oven-Fried Chicken," "Red Hot Fusilli,"
"Stir-Fried Beef and Potatoes," "Apricot-Orange Bread," "Crunchy
Pumpkin Pie," and a "Summer Breezes Smoothie."

The recipe collection was developed by the National Heart,
Lung, and Blood Institute (NHLBI) to help Americans keep their
heartbeat strong. It includes dishes from a variety of ethnic
cuisines to suit virtually every taste.

The dishes will even tempt children. That's important because
good eating habits need to start early. So, cook up some "Delicious
Oven French Fries" and teach your kids how good good health can
taste. Chances are, they'll want another lesson.

Besides recipes, the collection also offers information on special topics, such as how diet affects key factors involved in heart
health, how to use the Nutrition Facts Label, how to make healthier meals out of those old family favorites, why fiber matters, and
how to reduce salt and sodium in dishes. Check the table of contents for a listing of these topics.

You'll also find a list of certain nutrients for each recipe. This
list tells you how much the dish has of nutrients important to
health so you can keep track of your daily intakes. Page 6 offers
tips on how to use this information as part of your overall eating
plan. One such healthy eating plan, which comes from the
Dietary Guidelines for Americans, is outlined beginning on page 11.

If this collection sharpens your appetite to learn more about healthy eating or other heart-related topics, try another course. Here's how:

- Write to the NHLBI Health Information Center
  P.O. Box 30105
  Bethesda, MD 20824-0105
  Phone: (301) 592-8573
  TTY: (240) 629-3255
  Fax: (301) 592-8563

- Visit the NHLBI online at: **www.nhlbi.nih.gov**

Or, try these special NHLBI Web pages:

- For information about how to lose extra pounds or maintain a healthy weight: **www.nhlbi.nih.gov/health/public/heart/obesity/lose_wt**

- To learn about high blood pressure: **www.nhlbi.nih.gov/hbp**

- To learn about high blood cholesterol: **www.nhlbi.nih.gov/chd**

- To learn about heart health for women: **www.nhlbi.nih.gov/health/hearttruth**

Make a start today—and keep your heart as healthy as your appetite.

Eating for Heart Health—How Nutrition Affects Three Key Risk Factors

What you eat can help keep your heart beating strong—or lead to overweight, high blood pressure, and high blood cholesterol, three key factors that increase the risk of developing heart disease. (See the Box on page 5 for more on risk factors and heart disease.)

Here's a brief look at why these three risk factors are so important:

1. Overweight and Obesity

Overweight and obesity pose major health risks. First, they increase the risk of heart disease. Second, they make you more likely to develop other factors that also increase that risk. For instance, overweight and obesity increase your chance of developing high blood pressure and high blood cholesterol (see following sections), and diabetes—all major risk factors for heart disease.

So it's important to stay at a healthy weight. There's no gimmick to achieving this goal. The amount of calories you take in through your diet should not exceed the amount you expend through body metabolism and physical activities. If you eat more calories than you use up, you'll gain weight. But, even a small decrease in calories eaten can help keep you from gaining weight.

If you are overweight, losing just 10 percent of your current weight helps to lower your risk of heart disease. If you can't lose extra weight just yet, then try not to gain more.

Here are a few tips to help you keep your weight in check:

- Watch out for portion size. It's not just what you eat, but how much (see page 8).

- Choose fewer high-fat foods. These often have more calories than the same amount of other foods.

- But be careful of "lowfat" foods. They aren't always low in calories. Sometimes, extra sugars are added to lowfat items, such as desserts. They can be just as high in calories as regular versions.

- Be physically active—if you are, you've got a good chance of keeping your calorie equation in balance.

2. High Blood Pressure

Also called hypertension, this condition puts you at risk for heart disease and stroke. Diet plays a big role in your chance of developing high blood pressure. Following an eating plan low in saturated fat and cholesterol, and moderate in total fat is important for heart health generally and may help prevent or control high blood pressure. A key ingredient of this plan should be reducing your intake of salt (sodium chloride) and other forms of sodium.

Only small amounts of salt occur naturally in foods. Instead, most of the salt Americans consume is added during food processing, in preparation at home, or in a restaurant. By cutting back on salt, you'll probably lessen your taste for it over time.

Try to consume no more than 6 grams (about 1 teaspoon) of table salt a day. That equals 2.4 grams (2,400 milligrams) of sodium a day. Studies such as the *Dietary Approaches to Stop Hypertension* trial, or DASH, show that persons with or at an increased risk of developing high blood pressure can help control or prevent the condition by further reducing table salt—to 4 grams (or 2/3 teaspoon) a day. That equals 1.5 grams (1,500 milligrams) of sodium a day. Both totals include ALL salt and sodium consumed—that used in cooking and at the table, as well as in prepared foods.

3. High Blood Cholesterol

Fat and cholesterol in the diet can raise the level of cholesterol in the blood—and that can lead to atherosclerosis, a type of "hardening of the arteries." In atherosclerosis, cholesterol, fat, and other substances build up in artery walls. As the process continues, arteries, including those to the heart, may narrow, reducing blood flow.

Saturated fat raises blood cholesterol more than anything else in the diet. See page 19 for more about fat.

Help reduce your fat intake by looking for lowfat or fat free dairy products and other fat free items—but, again, keep an eye on the products' calorie content so you don't gain weight.

Some foods can actually help to lower blood cholesterol. This includes foods with soluble (also called viscous) fiber. Soluble fiber is found in cereal grains, fruits, vegetables, and legumes (which include beans, peas, and lentils). See page 18 for more on fiber.

Other food products also help lower blood cholesterol: These products contain plant stanols or plant sterols. These include cholesterol-lowering margarines. Plant stanols and sterols are noted on product food labels.

Reduce Your Heart Disease Risk

If you've got a heart, heart disease could be your problem. Heart disease affects women just as much as it does men. But everyone can take steps to reduce their chance of developing the disease.

How? By preventing or controlling behaviors and conditions known to increase its risk. They're called "risk factors," and there are two types—those you can change and those you can't. Luckily, most of them can be changed. These are smoking, high blood pressure, high blood cholesterol, overweight/obesity, physical inactivity, and diabetes.

Those you can't alter are your age (45 or older for men; 55 or older for women) and having a family history of early heart disease (a father or brother diagnosed before age 55, or a mother or sister diagnosed before age 65).

Start now to improve your heart-health profile. For instance, following a heart healthy eating plan helps prevent or control high blood pressure, high blood cholesterol, overweight, and diabetes. Here are some other steps you can take to help protect your heart health:

- **Stop smoking.** If you can't quit the first time, keep trying.

- **Lower high blood pressure.** Have your blood pressure checked regularly (once every 2 years if it is normal, more often if it is not). Also, maintain a healthy weight and limit your intake of alcoholic beverages—to one drink a day for women and two for men.

- **Reduce high blood cholesterol.** Maintain a healthy weight and get your cholesterol level checked once every 5 years (more often, if needed). The test measures the level of cholesterol circulating in the bloodstream.

- **Aim for a healthy weight.** To lose weight and keep it off, adopt a lifestyle that combines sensible eating with regular physical activity.

- **Be physically active.** Do at least 30 minutes of a moderate-intensity physical activity, such as brisk walking, on most and preferably all days of the week.

- **Prevent or manage diabetes.** The steps that lower your risk of heart disease also reduce your chance of developing diabetes. If you already have diabetes, be sure to manage it.

Planning a Nutritious Day

Eating well means enjoying a variety of food—and so does eating to stay well. Variety matters because no food has all the nutrients and other substances needed by your heart—and the rest of your body. So be sure to follow a well-balanced eating plan.

The nutrient list that accompanies the recipes in this collection can help you keep your diet in balance. The list gives nutrients vital for good heart health. Use the list to aim for the recommended daily total intakes of those nutrients.

The recommended daily intakes for healthy adults a[...]
below. Your needs may differ from these if you are over[...]
have heart disease, high blood pressure, high cholestero[...]
or another condition. If you do, check with your docto[...]
tian to find out what intakes are best for you.

Daily calorie and nutrient intakes:

● **Calories** ....Consume enough to stay at a healthy weight

A calorie is a unit of energy, not a nutrient. The amount that's best for you depends largely on your height and weight. You'll also need to consider whether or not you have to lose pounds. Other factors that affect your calorie needs include how physically active you are and your age. Physical activity helps burn calories, while middle-aged and older adults tend to need fewer calories than younger persons.

Typical daily intakes are:

1,600 calories—For young children (ages 2-6), women, and some older adults

2,200 calories—For older children, teenage girls, active women, and most men

2,800 calories—For teenage boys and active men

● **Total fat** ....No more than 30 percent of daily calories

● **Saturated fat** ......Less than 10 percent of daily calories

● **Cholesterol**.........Less than 300 milligrams per day

● **Fiber** ....25–30 grams per day

● **Protein** ....10–35 percent of daily calories

● **Carbohydrates**....45–65 percent of daily calories

● **Sodium** ....No more than 2,400 milligrams per day

...o calculate percent of daily calories, it's important to know
...at protein and carbohydrate have 4 calories per gram, while fat
has 9 calories per gram. So, for example, if you eat 2,000 calories
a day, your daily total intakes should be: no more than 67 grams
of total fat, 22 grams or less of saturated fat, and 225–325 grams of
carbohydrates. For the other nutrients, have no more than the
maximums listed above. The Box on page 20 gives some daily
totals for saturated fat and total fat.

However, try to remember that the goal is to build a nutritious
pattern from nutritious meals. Not every dish needs to be low in
fat or calories. Keep your sights set on an overall healthy pattern.

Don't Ignore Portion Size

When it comes to heart health, size matters. It's very easy to "eat
with your eyes" and misjudge what equals a portion. That makes
it just as easy to pile on unwanted pounds. So be sure you eat a
sensible portion size. The recipes in this collection are designed to
give you a satisfying portion.

**Take advantage of two other good sources of information about
portion size:**

- *Nutrition and Your Health: Dietary Guidelines for Americans*—See
  "A Pyramid of Healthy Foods," which begins on page 11. The
  section gives the portion sizes used in this healthy eating plan.

- Nutrition Facts Label—The section that begins on page 9 tells
  how to read these labels, which give calorie and nutrient contents
  per serving. Products often are sold as single portions but actually
  contain more than one serving. For instance, a small bag of
  pretzels may be sold as one portion but contain two servings. Be
  especially careful of portion size when choosing high-calorie items.

Let the Nutrition Facts Label Guide You to Healthy Choices

Shopping for the right food item can be dizzying. Shelves are packed with different brands, some with special health claims.

There's a surefire way to pick out the best item: Read its Nutrition Facts Label. This label gives you x-ray eyes. It tells you nutritional value and number of servings in an item.

The label has another asset too—the Percent Daily Value listing. This tells you how much each serving of the item supplies of the day's recommended intake for total fat, saturated fat, cholesterol, sodium, total carbohydrate, dietary fiber, vitamins A and C, calcium, and iron. Not bad.

Use the Nutrition Facts Label to compare foods. As a guide, if you want to consume more of a nutrient (such as fiber), try to choose foods with a higher Percent Daily Value; to consume less of a nutrient (such as saturated fat, cholesterol, or sodium), choose foods with a lower Percent Daily Value. Try the "5–20" guide—an easy way to use the Percent Daily Value to compare the nutrients in similar foods. So, for nutrients

Nutrition Facts

Serving Size 1/2 cup (67g)
Servings Per Container 16

Amount Per Serving

Calories 100	Calories from Fat 0

	% Daily Value
Total Fat 0g	0%
Saturated Fat 0g	0%
Cholesterol 0g	0%
Sodium 60mg	3%
Total Carbohydrate 22g	7%
Dietary Fiber 0g	0%
Sugars 15g	
Protein 3g	

Vitamin A	2%	Vitamin C*	0%
Calcium	45%	Iron*	0%

*Percent Daily Values are based on a 2,000 calorie diet.

you want to get less of, look for a Percent Daily Value of 5 or less; for nutrients you want to have more of, look for a Percent Daily Value of 20 or more.

Also get in the habit of checking an item's ingredient list. It will tell you what's in the food—including any added nutrients, fats, or sugars. Ingredients are listed in descending order of amount by weight.

See the Box below for information on how to decipher the special content claims on food labels.

Learn the Label Language

One of the best ways to find heart healthy products is to check food labels. Here are some terms to look for when choosing low-sodium, lowfat, and low-calorie items:

PHRASE	WHAT IT MEANS
FOR SODIUM	
Sodium free or salt free	Less than 5 milligrams per serving
Very low sodium	35 milligrams or less per serving
Low sodium	140 milligrams or less per serving
Low sodium meal	140 milligrams or less per 3 1/2 ounces (100 grams)
Reduced or less sodium	At least 25 percent less sodium than the regular version
Light in sodium	Half the sodium of the regular version
Unsalted or no salt added	No salt added to the product during processing

A Pyramid of Healthy Foods

If you're searching for a healthy overall eating plan, you've come to the right page. The Federal Government has created a pyramid to good health—in fact, it's called the "Food Guide Pyramid."

The idea is that the base of the pyramid forms the foundation for good nutrition and the foods you should eat most often. As you go up the pyramid, you eat less of the major food groups represented. Putting all the pyramid's groups together assures you a well-rounded diet. The pyramid's also designed to encourage you to choose a variety of foods from within the groups.

PHRASE	WHAT IT MEANS
FOR FATS	
Fat free	Less than 0.5 grams per serving
Low saturated fat	1 gram or less per serving
Lowfat	3 grams or less per serving
Reduced fat	At least 25 percent less fat than the regular version
Light in fat	Half the fat of the regular version
FOR CALORIES	
Calorie free	Less than 5 calories per serving
Low calorie	40 calories or less per serving
Reduced or less calories	At least 25 percent fewer calories than the regular version
Light or lite	Half the fat or a third of the calories of the regular version

le Pyramid
Y FOOD CHOICES

KEY

Fat (naturally occurring and added)

Sugars (added)

These symbols show fat and added sugars in food.

weets
LY

Milk, Yogurt, and Cheese Group
2-3 SERVINGS

Meat, Poultry, Fish, Dry Beans, Eggs, and Nuts Group
2-3 SERVINGS

Fruit Group
2-4 SERVINGS

Vegetable Group
3-5 SERVINGS

Bread, Cereal, Rice, and Pasta Group
6-11 SERVINGS

The pyramid is shown above, along with the recommended daily servings. More information about the servings appears below.

What Counts as a Serving?

There's one more piece of vital information you need to follow the pyramid, and that's what counts as a serving. Here are some examples of one serving of each of the pyramid's building blocks:

● **Bread, Cereal, Rice, and Pasta (Grains Group)—especially whole grain**

1 slice bread

About 1 cup of ready-to-eat cereal

$^1/_2$ cup of cooked cereal, rice, or pasta

- **Vegetable Group**

  1 cup of raw leafy vegetables

  $^1/_2$ cup of other vegetables—cooked or raw

  $^3/_4$ cup of vegetable juice

- **Fruit Group**

  1 medium apple, banana, orange, pear

  $^1/_2$ cup of chopped, cooked, or canned fruit

  $^3/_4$ cup of fruit juice

- **Milk, Yogurt, and Cheese (Milk Group)—preferably fat free or lowfat**

  1 cup of milk or yogurt

  $1^1/_2$ ounces of natural cheese (such as Cheddar)

  2 ounces of processed cheese (such as American)

- **Meat, Poultry, Fish, Dry Beans, Eggs, and Nuts (Meat and Beans Group)—preferably lean or lowfat**

  2–3 ounces of cooked lean meat, poultry, or fish

  $^1/_2$ cup of cooked dry beans or $^1/_2$ cup of tofu—these count as 1 ounce of lean meat

  > *(Note: Dry beans, peas, and lentils can be counted as servings in either the meat and beans group or the vegetable group. As a vegetable, $^1/_2$ cup of cooked, dry beans counts as one serving. As a meat substitute, 1 cup of cooked, dry beans counts as one serving—2 ounces of meat.)*

  $2^1/_2$–ounce soyburger or 1 egg counts as 1 ounce of lean meat

  2 tablespoons of peanut butter or $^1/_3$ cup of nuts counts as 1 ounce of meat

Keeping the "Heart" in Old Family Favorites

Eating heart healthy meals doesn't mean giving up some of those too-rich favorite family recipes. With a few changes, you can keep the heart and add the health. Here's how:

General Substitutions

Milk/Cream/Sour Cream

● Cook with lowfat (1 percent fat) or fat free dry or evaporated milk, instead of whole milk or cream.

● Instead of sour cream, blend 1 cup lowfat, unsalted cottage cheese with 1 tablespoon fat free milk and 2 tablespoons lemon juice, or substitute plain, fat free or lowfat yogurt or sour cream.

Spices/Flavorings

● Use a variety of herbs and spices in place of salt (see page 17).

● Use low-sodium bouillon and broths, instead of regular bouillons and broths.

● Use a small amount of skinless smoked turkey breast, instead of fatback to lower fat content but keep taste.

● Use skinless chicken thighs, instead of neck bones.

Oils/Butter

● Use cooking oil spray to lower fat and calories.

● Use a small amount of vegetable oil, instead of lard, butter, or other fats that are hard at room temperature.

- In general, diet margarines are not well suited for baking. Instead, to cut saturated fat, use regular soft margarine made with vegetable oil.

- Choose margarine that lists liquid vegetable oil as the first ingredient on the food label.

Eggs

- In baking or cooking, use 3 egg whites and 1 egg yolk, instead of 2 whole eggs, or 2 egg whites or 1/4 cup of egg substitute, instead of 1 whole egg.

For Meats and Poultry

- Choose a lean cut of meat (see page 22) and remove any visible fat.

- Remove skin from chicken and other poultry before cooking.

For Sandwiches and Salads

- In salads and sandwiches, use fat free or lowfat dressing, yogurt, or mayonnaise, instead of regular versions.

- To make a salad dressing, use equal parts water and vinegar, and half as much oil.

- Garnish salads with fruits and vegetables.

For Soups and Stews

- Remove fat from homemade broths, soups, and stews by preparing them ahead and chilling them. Before reheating the dish, lift off the hardened fat that formed at the surface. If you don't have time to chill the dish, then float a few ice cubes on the surface of the warm liquid to harden the fat. Then, remove and discard the fat.

- Use cooking spray, water, or stock to sauté onion for flavoring stews, soups, and sauces.

For Breads

- To make muffins, quick breads, and biscuits, use no more than 1–2 tablespoons of fat for each cup of flour.

- When making muffins or quick breads, use three ripe, very well-mashed bananas, instead of 1/2 cup butter or oil. Or, substitute a cup of applesauce for a cup of butter, margarine, oil, or shortening—you'll get less saturated fat and fewer calories.

For Desserts

- To make a pie crust, use only 1/2 cup margarine for every 2 cups flour.

- For chocolate desserts, use 3 tablespoons of cocoa, instead of 1 ounce of baking chocolate. If fat is needed to replace that in chocolate, add 1 tablespoon or less of vegetable oil.

- To make cakes and soft-drop cookies, use no more than 2 tablespoons of fat for each cup of flour.

Making Mealtimes Spicy

Less fat? Less salt? How can you do that and get more taste?
Easy. Flavor with spices and herbs.

Here's a rundown of what goes best with what:

For Meat, Poultry, and Fish

Beef ....Bay leaf, marjoram, nutmeg, onion, pepper, sage,
thyme

Lamb..................Curry powder, garlic, rosemary, mint

Pork...................Garlic, onion, sage, pepper, oregano

Vea ....Bay leaf, curry powder, ginger, marjoram, oregano

Chicken ....Ginger, marjoram, oregano, paprika, poultry
seasoning, rosemary, sage, tarragon, thyme

Fish...................Curry powder, dill, dry mustard, lemon juice,
marjoram, paprika, pepper

For Vegetables

Carrots ....Cinnamon, cloves, marjoram, nutmeg, rosemary,
sage

Corn...................Cumin, curry powder, onion, paprika, parsley

Green beans ....Dill, curry powder, lemon juice, marjoram,
oregano, tarragon, thyme

Greens................Onion, pepper

Peas ....Ginger, marjoram, onion, parsley, sage

Potatoes ....Dill, garlic, onion, paprika, parsley, sage

Summer squash ..Cloves, curry powder, marjoram, nutmeg, rosemary, sage

Winter squash ....Cinnamon, ginger, nutmeg, onion

Tomatoes ....Basil, bay leaf, dill, marjoram, onion, oregano, parsley, pepper

Fast Facts on Fiber, Fat, and Salt

That it? You say you still have questions? Thought so. Here are a few quick facts and tips on fiber, fat, and sodium.

Fiber—Why Does It Matter, and What Is It Anyway?

You've probably heard that it's good to eat plenty of fiber. But what is fiber, and why is it important for your heart?

Fiber comes from plants. Since your body can't really digest fiber or absorb it into your bloodstream, it's not nourished by it. That means, technically speaking, fiber isn't a "nutrient." But it's vital for good health.

First, fiber can help reduce your risk of heart disease. Second, it's also good for the digestive tract and overall health. And, as a bonus, eating lots of fiber helps you feel full on fewer calories, which makes it ideal if you're trying to lose weight.

There are two main types of fiber—soluble (also called "viscous") and insoluble. While both have health benefits, only soluble fiber reduces the risk of heart disease.

The difference between the types is how they go through the digestive track. Soluble fiber mixes with liquid and binds to fatty substances to help remove them from the body. Soluble fiber thus helps to lower cholesterol levels—thereby reducing the risk of heart disease. Good sources of soluble fiber are whole oats, barley, fruits, vegetables, and legumes (which include beans, peas, and lentils).

Insoluble fiber goes through the digestive tract largely un-solved. Also called "roughage," insoluble fiber helps the colon function properly. Good sources of insoluble fiber are whole-grain foods (such as wheat and corn bran), fruits (such as apples and pears with the skins), vegetables (such as green beans, cauliflower, and potatoes with the skins), and legumes.

As you can see, many foods have both soluble and insoluble fiber. As a rule, fruits have more soluble fiber and vegetables more insoluble fiber.

You should try to eat 25–30 grams of total fiber each day. That should include at least 5–10 grams daily of soluble fiber.

Here's a more complete list of good sources of soluble fiber:

- **Whole grain cereals and seeds**—barley; oatmeal; oatbran; and psyllium seeds (ground)

- **Fruits**—apples (with the skin); bananas; blackberries; citrus (such as oranges and grapefruits); nectarines; peaches; pears; plums; and prunes

- **Legumes**—black, kidney, lima, navy, northern, and pinto beans; yellow, green, and orange lentils; and chickpeas and black-eyed peas

- **Vegetables**—broccoli; brussels sprouts; and carrots

Fat—Isn't It Always Bad for You?

Fat is a nutrient that helps the body function in various ways: For example, it supplies the body with energy. It also helps other nutrients work and, when it becomes fatty tissue, it protects organs and provides insulation, keeping you warm. But the body only needs small amounts of fat. Too much fat can have bad effects, including turning into unwanted excess pounds and increasing cholesterol in the bloodstream (see page 4).

ifferent types of fat, and they have different effects
f heart disease. Knowing which fat does what can
ose healthier foods.

owdown on fats:

● **Total fat.** This is the sum of saturated, monounsaturated, and
polyunsaturated fats and trans fatty acids in food. Foods have
a varying mix of these three types.

Figuring Your Fat

Each day, aim for intakes of less than 10 percent of calories from
saturated fat and no more than 30 percent of calories from total fat.
Those are the recommended daily intakes for healthy adults.

Here are some examples of the maximum amount of fat you should
consume:

If you consume: Calories a Day	Eat no nore than: Saturated Fat	Total Fat
1,200	13 grams	40 grams
1,600	18 grams	53 grams
2,000*	22 grams	67 grams
2,200	24 grams	73 grams
2,500*	28 grams	83 grams
2,800	31 grams	93 grams

* Percent Daily Values on Nutrition Facts Labels are based on a 2,000 calorie diet.
Values for 2,000 and 2,500 calories are rounded to the nearest 5 grams to be
consistent with the Nutrients Facts Label.

- **Saturated fat.** This fat is usually solid at room and refrigerator temperatures. It is found in greatest amounts in foods from animals, such as fatty cuts of meat, poultry with the skin, whole-milk dairy products, lard, and some vegetable oils, including coconut and palm oils. Saturated fat increases cholesterol in the blood more than anything else in the diet. Keep your intake of saturated fat low.

- **Unsaturated fat.** This fat is usually liquid at room and refrigerator temperatures. Unsaturated fats occur in vegetable oils, most nuts, olives, avocados, and fatty fish, such as salmon.

  There are types of unsaturated fat—monounsaturated and polyunsaturated. When used instead of saturated fat, monounsaturated and polyunsaturated fats help lower blood cholesterol levels. Monounsaturated fat is found in greatest amounts in foods from plants, including olive, canola, sunflower, and peanut oils. Polyunsaturated fat is found in greatest amounts in foods from plants, including safflower, sunflower, corn, soybean, and cottonseed oils, and many kinds of nuts. A type of polyunsaturated fat is called omega-3 fatty acids, which are being studied to see if they help guard against heart disease. Good sources of omega-3 fatty acids are some fish, such as salmon, tuna, and mackerel.

  Use moderate amounts of food high in unsaturated fats, taking care to avoid excess calories.

- **Trans fatty acids.** Foods high in trans fatty acids tend to raise blood cholesterol. These foods include those high in partially hydrogenated vegetable oils, such as many hard margarines and shortenings. Foods with a high amount of these ingredients include some commercially fried foods and some bakery goods.

The Box on pages 10–11 can help you choose foods lower in fat. The Box on page 20 gives examples of how much saturated fat and total fat you should consume daily.

Are Some Cuts of Meat Less Fatty Than Others?

Definitely. Here's a guide to the lower-fat cuts:

Beef ....Top round, eye of round, round steak, rump roast, sirloin tip, short loin, strip steak lean, lean and extra lean ground beef

Pork.....................Tenderloin, sirloin roast or chop, center cut loin chops

Lamb...................Foreshank, leg roast, leg chop, loin chop

What's the Best Way To Cook To Reduce Fat?

You're in luck. There's a host of lowfat cooking methods. Try these—but remember not to add butter or high-fat sauces:

- Bake
- Broil
- Microwave
- Roast
- Steam
- Poach
- Lightly stir fry or sauté in cooking spray, small amount of vegetable oil, or reduced sodium broth
- Grill seafood, chicken, or vegetables

Salt—How Can I Reduce the Amount of Salt I Eat?

Most Americans eat too much salt (sodium chloride). You can help protect yourself against high blood pressure—and so heart disease and stroke—by reducing the amount of salt and other forms of sodium in your diet. As noted on pages 4 and 7, try to consume no more than 2,400 milligrams of sodium a day—or, if you can, 1,500 milligrams a day. That includes all the salt and sodium in your diet, whether added at the table or in cooking, or already in processed foods. The Box on pages 10–11 offers advice on how to use food labels to find lower sodium products.

Here are some tips on ways you can reduce your intake of salt and sodium:

● Use reduced sodium or no salt added products. For example, choose low- or reduced-sodium, or no salt added versions of foods and condiments when available.

● Buy fresh, frozen, or canned "with no salt added" vegetables.

● Use fresh poultry, fish, and lean meat, rather than canned, smoked, or processed types.

● Choose ready-to-eat breakfast cereals that are lower in sodium.

● Limit cured foods (such as bacon and ham), foods packed in brine (such as pickles, pickled vegetables, olives, and sauer-kraut), and condiments (such as MSG, horseradish, catsup, and barbecue sauce). Limit even lower sodium versions of soy sauce and teriyaki sauce—treat these condiments as you do table salt.

● Be spicy instead of salty. In cooking and at the table, flavor foods with herbs, spices, lemon, lime, vinegar, or salt-free sea-soning blends.

- Cook rice, pasta, and hot cereals without salt. Cut back on instant or flavored rice, pasta, and cereal mixes, which usually have added salt.

- Choose "convenience" foods that are lower in sodium. Cut back on frozen dinners, mixed dishes such as pizza, packaged mixes, canned soups or broths, and salad dressings—these often have a lot of sodium.

- Rinse canned foods, such as tuna, to remove some sodium.

RECIPES

ABBREVIATIONS

Recipes use the following abbreviations:

C .... cup

lb .... pound

oz .... ounce

pt .... pint

qt .... quart

Tbsp .... tablespoon

tsp .... teaspoon

Nutrient lists use the following abbreviations:

g .... gram

mg .... milligram

% .... percent

Appetizers and Soups

Bean and Macaroni Soup

This satisfying dish is virtually fat free—it uses just 1 tablespoon of oil for 16 servings.

2 cans	(16 oz each) great northern beans
1 Tbsp	olive oil
1/2 lb	fresh mushrooms, sliced
1 C	onion, coarsely chopped
2 C	carrots, sliced
1 C	celery, coarsely chopped
1 clove	garlic, minced
3 C	tomatoes, fresh, peeled, cut up (or 1 1/2 lb canned, whole, cut up)*
1 tsp	dried sage
1 tsp	dried thyme
1/2 tsp	dried oregano
to taste	black pepper, freshly ground
1	bay leaf, crumbled
4 C	elbow macaroni, cooked

*If using canned tomatoes, sodium content will be higher. Try no salt added canned tomatoes to keep sodium lower.

Yield: 16 servings
Serving size: 1 cup
Each serving provides:
Calories: 158
Total fat: 1 g
Saturated fat: less than 1 g
Cholesterol: 0 mg
Sodium: 154 mg
Total fiber: 5 mg
Protein: 8 mg
Carbohydrates: 29 g
Potassium: 524 mg

1. Drain beans and reserve liquid. Rinse beans.

2. Heat oil in 6-quart kettle. Add mushrooms, onion, carrots, celery, and garlic and sauté for 5 minutes.

3. Add tomatoes, sage, thyme, oregano, pepper, and bay leaf. Cover and cook over medium heat for 20 minutes.

4. Cook macaroni according to directions on package, using unsalted water. Drain when cooked. Do not overcook.

5. Combine reserved bean liquid with water to make 4 cups.

6. Add liquid, beans, and cooked macaroni to vegetable mixture.

7. Bring to boil. Cover and simmer until soup is thoroughly heated. Stir occasionally.

Cannery Row Soup

Fish and clam juice give this soup a hearty taste of the sea.

2 lb	varied fish fillets (such as haddock, perch, flounder, cod, sole), cut into 1-inch cubes
2 Tbsp	olive oil
1 clove	garlic, minced
3	carrots, cut in thin strips
2 C	celery, sliced
$1/2$ C	onion, chopped
$1/4$ C	green peppers, chopped
1 can	(28 oz) whole tomatoes, cut up, with liquid
1 C	clam juice
$1/4$ tsp	dried thyme, crushed
$1/4$ tsp	dried basil, crushed
$1/8$ tsp	black pepper
$1/4$ C	fresh parsley, minced

1. Heat oil in large saucepan. Sauté garlic, carrots, celery, onion, and green pepper in oil for 3 minutes.

2. Add remaining ingredients, except parsley and fish. Cover and simmer for 10–15 minutes or until vegetables are fork tender.

3. Add fish and parsley. Simmer covered for 5–10 minutes more or until fish flakes easily and is opaque. Serve hot.

Yield: 8 servings
Serving size: 1 cup
Each serving provides:
Calories: 170
Total fat: 5 g
Saturated fat: less than 1 g
Cholesterol: 56 mg
Sodium: 380 mg
Total fiber: 3 g
Protein: 22 g
Carbohydrates: 9 g
Potassium: 710 mg

Corn Chowder

Here's a creamy chowder without the cream—or fat.

1 Tbsp	vegetable oil
2 Tbsp	celery, finely diced
2 Tbsp	onion, finely diced
2 Tbsp	green pepper, finely diced
1 package	(10 oz) frozen whole kernel corn
1 C	raw potatoes, peeled, diced in 1/2-inch pieces
2 Tbsp	fresh parsley, chopped
1 C	water
1/4 tsp	salt
to taste	black pepper
1/4 tsp	paprika
2 Tbsp	flour
2 C	lowfat or skim milk

1. Heat oil in medium saucepan. Add celery, onion, and green pepper, and sauté for 2 minutes.

2. Add corn, potatoes, water, salt, pepper, and paprika. Bring to boil, then reduce heat to medium. Cook covered for about 10 minutes or until potatoes are tender.

3. Place 1/2 cup of milk in jar with tight-fitting lid. Add flour and shake vigorously.

4. Gradually add milk-flour mixture to cooked vegetables. Then add remaining milk.

5. Cook, stirring constantly, until mixture comes to boil and thickens. Serve garnished with chopped, fresh parsley.

Yield: 4 servings
Serving size: 1 cup
Each serving provides:
Calories: 186
Total fat: 5 g
Saturated fat: 1 g
Cholesterol: 5 mg
Sodium: 205 mg
Total fiber: 4 g
Protein: 7 g
Carbohydrates: 31 g
Potassium: 455 mg

Curtido (Cabbage) Salvadoreño

Surprise your taste buds with this flavorful dish— esta terrifica!

1	medium head cabbage, chopped
2	small carrots, grated
1	small onion, sliced
$^1/_2$ tsp	dried red pepper (optional)
$^1/_2$ tsp	oregano
1 tsp	olive oil
1 tsp	salt
1 tsp	brown sugar
$^1/_2$ C	vinegar
$^1/_2$ C	water

►SERVING TIP

Try this dish with Pupusas Revueltas (see page 37).

1. Blanch cabbage with boiling water for 1 minute. Discard water.

2. Place cabbage in large bowl and add grated carrots, sliced onion, red pepper, oregano, olive oil, salt, brown sugar, vinegar, and water.

3. Place in refrigerator for at least 2 hours before serving.

Yield: 8 servings
Serving size: 1 cup
Each serving provides:
Calories: 41
Total fat: 1 g
Saturated fat: less than 1 g
Cholesterol: 0 mg
Sodium: 293 mg
Total fiber: 2 g
Protein: 2 g
Carbohydrates: 7 g
Potassium: 325 mg

cho

This chilled tomato soup is a classic—and chock full of healthy garden-fresh vegetables.

3	medium tomatoes, peeled, chopped
$1/2$ C	cucumber, seeded, chopped
$1/2$ C	green pepper, chopped
2	green onions, sliced
2 C	low-sodium vegetable juice cocktail
1 Tbsp	lemon juice
$1/2$ tsp	basil, dried
$1/4$ tsp	hot pepper sauce
1 clove	garlic, minced

1. In large mixing bowl, combine all ingredients.
2. Cover and chill in the refrigerator for several hours.

Yield: 4 servings
Serving size: 1$1/4$ cups
Each serving provides:
Calories: 52
Total fat: less than 1 g
Saturated fat: less than 1 g
Cholesterol: 0 mg
Sodium: 41 mg
Total fiber: 2 g
Protein: 2 g
Carbohydrates: 12 g
Potassium: 514 mg

Homemade Turkey Soup

This popular soup uses a "quick cool down" that lets you skim the fat right off the top—making it even healthier.

6 lb	turkey breast with bones (with at least 2 C meat)
2	medium onions
3 stalks	celery
1 tsp	dried thyme
$1/2$ tsp	dried rosemary
$1/2$ tsp	dried sage
1 tsp	dried basil
$1/2$ tsp	dried marjoram
$1/2$ tsp	dried tarragon
$1/2$ tsp	salt
to taste	black pepper
$1/2$ lb	Italian pastina or pasta

**Yield: 16 servings
(about 4 quarts of soup)
Serving size: 1 cup
Each serving provides:**
Calories: 201
Total fat: 2 g
Saturated fat: 1 g
Cholesterol: 101 mg
Sodium: 141 mg
Total fiber: 1 g
Protein: 33 g
Carbohydrates: 11 g
Potassium: 344 mg

1. Place turkey breast in large 6-quart pot. Cover with water until at least three-quarters full.

2. Peel onions, cut into large pieces, and add to pot. Wash celery stalks, slice, and add to pot.

3. Simmer covered for about $2^1/2$ hours.

4. Remove carcass from pot. Divide soup into smaller, shallower containers for quick cooling in refrigerator.

5. After cooling, skim off fat.

6. While soup cools, remove remaining meat from turkey carcass. Cut into pieces.

7. Add turkey meat to skimmed soup, along with herbs and spices.

8. Bring to boil and add pastina. Continue cooking on low boil for about 20 minutes, until pastina is done. Serve at once or refrigerate for later reheating.

Meatball Soup

This soup beefs up the health by using chicken with lean beef to lower the fat.

1/2 lb	ground chicken
1/2 lb	ground lean beef
10 C	water
1 Tbsp	annato (also called achiote), optional, for coloring
1	bay leaf
1	small onion, chopped
1/2 C	green pepper, chopped
1 tsp	mint
2	small tomatoes, chopped
1/2 tsp	oregano
4 Tbsp	instant corn flour
1/2 tsp	black pepper
2 cloves	garlic, minced
1/2 tsp	salt
2	medium carrots, chopped
2 C	cabbage, chopped
2	celery stalks, chopped
1 package	(10 oz) frozen corn
2	medium zucchini, chopped
1	medium chayote, chopped (added zucchini can be used instead)
1/2 C	cilantro, minced

Yield: 8 servings
Serving size: 1 1/4 cups
Each serving provides:
Calories: 161
Total fat: 4 g
Saturated fat: 1 g
Cholesterol: 31 mg
Sodium: 193 mg
Total fiber: 4 g
Protein: 13 g
Carbohydrates: 17 g
Potassium: 461 mg

1. In large pot, combine water, annato, bay leaf, half of onion, green pepper, and 1/2 teaspoon of mint. Bring to boil.

2. In bowl, combine chicken, beef, other half of onion, tomato, oregano, corn flour, pepper, garlic, and salt. Mix well. Form 1-inch meatballs. Place meatballs in boiling water and lower heat. Cook over low heat for 30–45 minutes.

3. Add carrots, chayote, cabbage, and celery. Cook over low heat for 25 minutes. Add corn and zucchini. Cook for another 5 minutes. Garnish with cilantro and rest of mint.

Mexican Pozole

Try a change of taste with this hearty Mexican soup.

2 lb	lean beef, cubed*
1 Tbsp	olive oil
1	large onion, chopped
1	clove garlic, finely chopped
$1/4$ tsp	salt
$1/8$ tsp	pepper
$1/4$ C	cilantro
1 can	(15 oz) stewed tomatoes
2 oz	tomato paste
1 can	(1 lb 13 oz) hominy

*Skinless, boneless chicken breasts can be used instead of beef cubes.

1. In large pot, heat oil, then sauté beef.

2. Add onion, garlic, salt, pepper, cilantro, and enough water to cover meat. Cover pot and cook over low heat until meat is tender.

3. Add tomatoes and tomato paste. Continue cooking for about 20 minutes.

4. Add hominy and continue cooking over low heat for another 15 minutes, stirring occasionally. If too thick, add water for desired consistency.

Yield: 10 servings
Serving size: 1 cup
Each serving provides:
Calories: 253
Total fat: 10 g
Saturated fat: 3 g
Cholesterol: 52 mg
Sodium: 425 mg
Total fiber: 4 g
Protein: 22 g
Carbohydrates: 19 g
Potassium: 485 mg

Minestrone Soup

This cholesterol-free version of the classic Italian soup is brimming with fiber-rich beans, peas, and carrots.

$1/4$ C	olive oil
1 clove	garlic, minced (or $1/8$ tsp powder)
$1 1/3$ C	onion, coarsely chopped
$1 1/2$ C	celery with leaves, coarsely chopped
1 can	(6 oz) tomato paste
1 Tbsp	fresh parsley, chopped
1 C	carrots, sliced, fresh or frozen
$4 3/4$ C	cabbage, shredded
1 can	(1 lb) tomatoes, cut up
1 C	canned red kidney beans, drained, rinsed
$1 1/2$ C	frozen peas
$1 1/2$ C	fresh green beans
dash	hot sauce
11 C	water
2 C	spaghetti, uncooked, broken

1. Heat oil in 4-quart saucepan. Add garlic, onion, and celery, and sauté for about 5 minutes.

2. Add all remaining ingredients except spaghetti. Stir until ingredients are well mixed.

3. Bring to boil and reduce heat, cover, and simmer for about 45 minutes or until vegetables are tender.

4. Add uncooked spaghetti and simmer for only 2–3 minutes.

Yield: 16 servings
Serving Size: 1 cup
Each serving provides:
Calories: 112
Total fat: 4 g
Saturated fat: 0 g
Cholesterol: 0 mg
Sodium: 202 mg
Total fiber: 4 g
Protein: 4 g
Carbohydrates: 17 g
Potassium: 393 mg

Pupusas Revueltas

1 lb	chicken breast, ground
1 Tbsp	vegetable oil
1/2 lb	lowfat mozzarella cheese, grated
1/2	small onion, finely diced
1 clove	garlic, minced
1	medium green pepper, seeded, minced
1	small tomato, finely chopped
1/2 tsp	salt
5 C	instant corn flour (masa harina)
6 C	water

Ground chicken and lowfat cheese help keep down the fat and calories in this tasty dish.

▶SERVING TIP

Try this dish with Curtido Salvadoreño (see page 31).

1. In nonstick skillet, sauté chicken in oil over low heat until it turns white. Stir chicken constantly to keep it from sticking.

2. Add onion, garlic, green pepper, and tomato. Cook chicken mixture through. Remove skillet from stove and let mixture cool in refrigerator.

3. Meanwhile, place flour in large mixing bowl and stir in enough water to make stiff, tortilla-like dough.

4. When chicken mixture has cooled, mix in cheese.

5. Divide dough into 24 portions. With your hands, roll dough into balls and flatten each into 1/2–inch thick circle. Put spoonful of chicken mixture in middle of each circle of dough and bring edges to center. Flatten ball of dough again until it is 1/2–inch thick.

6. In very hot iron skillet, cook pupusas on each side until golden brown. Serve hot.

Yield: 12 servings
Serving size: 2 pupusas
Each serving provides:
Calories: 290
Total fat: 7 g
Saturated fat: 3 g
Cholesterol: 33 mg
Sodium: 223 mg
Total fiber: 5 g
Protein: 14 g
Carbohydrates: 38 g
Potassium: 272 mg

Rockport Fish Chowder

Serve this chowder as an appetizer or meal in itself—and eat like an admiral on a health cruise.

2 Tbsp	vegetable oil
1/4 C	onion, coarsely chopped
1/2 C	celery, coarsely chopped
1 C	carrots, sliced
2 C	potatoes, raw, peeled, cubed
1/4 tsp	thyme
1/2 tsp	paprika
2 C	bottled clam juice
8	whole peppercorns
1	bay leaf
1 lb	fresh or frozen (and thawed) cod or haddock fillets, cut into 3/4–inch cubes
1/4 C	flour
3 C	lowfat milk
1 Tbsp	fresh parsley, chopped

Yield: 8 servings
Serving size: 1 cup
Each serving provides:
Calories: 186
Total fat: 6 g
Saturated fat: 1 g
Cholesterol: 34 mg
Sodium: 302 mg
Total fiber: 2 g
Protein: 15 g
Carbohydrates: 18 g
Potassium: 602 mg

1. Heat oil in large saucepan. Add onion and celery, and sauté for about 3 minutes.

2. Add carrots, potatoes, thyme, paprika, and clam broth. Wrap peppercorns and bay leaf in cheese cloth. Add to pot. Bring to boil, reduce heat, and simmer for 15 minutes, then add fish and simmer for an added 15 minutes, or until fish flakes easily and is opaque.

3. Remove fish and vegetables. Break fish into chunks. Bring broth to boil and continue boiling until volume is reduced to 1 cup. Remove bay leaf and peppercorns.

4. Shake flour and 1/2 cup lowfat milk in container with tight-fitting lid until smooth. Add to broth in saucepan, along with remaining milk. Cook over medium heat, stirring constantly, until mixture boils and is thickened.

5. Return vegetables and fish chunks to stock and heat thoroughly. Serve hot, sprinkled with chopped parsley.

MAIN DISHES

Bavarian Beef

This classic German stew is made with lean, trimmed beef stew meat and cabbage.

1 1/4 lb	lean beef stew meat, trimmed of fat, cut in 1-inch pieces
1 Tbsp	vegetable oil
1	large onion, thinly sliced
1 1/2 C	water
3/4 tsp	caraway seeds
1/2 tsp	salt
1/8 tsp	black pepper
1	bay leaf
1/4 C	white vinegar
1 Tbsp	sugar
1/2	small head red cabbage, cut into 4 wedges
1/4 C	gingersnaps, crushed

1. Brown meat in oil in heavy skillet. Remove meat and sauté onion in remaining oil until golden. Return meat to skillet. Add water, caraway seeds, salt, pepper, and bay leaf. Bring to boil. Reduce heat, cover, and simmer for 1 1/4 hours.

2. Add vinegar and sugar, and stir. Place cabbage on top of meat. Cover and simmer for an added 45 minutes.

3. Remove meat and cabbage, arrange on platter, and keep warm.

4. Strain drippings from skillet and skim off fat. Add enough water to drippings to yield 1 cup of liquid.

5. Return to skillet with crushed gingersnaps. Cook and stir until thickened and mixture boils. Pour over meat and vegetables, and serve.

Yield: 5 servings
Serving size: 5 oz
Each serving provides:
Calories: 218
Total fat: 7 g
Saturated fat: 2 g
Cholesterol: 60 mg
Sodium: 323 mg
Total fiber: 2 g
Protein: 24 g
Carbohydrates: 14 g
Potassium: 509 mg

Beef and Bean Chili

Here's a lower fat chili that's lost none of its heat.

2 lb	lean beef stew meat, trimmed of fat, cut in 1-inch cubes
3 Tbsp	vegetable oil
2 C	water
2 tsp	garlic, minced
1	large onion, finely chopped
1 Tbsp	flour
2 tsp	chili powder
1	green pepper, chopped
2 lb	(or 3 C) tomatoes, chopped
1 Tbsp	oregano
1 tsp	cumin
2 C	canned kidney beans*

*To cut back on sodium, try using "no salt added" canned kidney beans or beans prepared at home without salt.

1. Brown meat in large skillet with half of vegetable oil. Add water. Simmer covered for 1 hour until meat is tender.

2. Heat remaining vegetable oil in second skillet. Add garlic and onion, and cook over low heat until onion is softened. Add flour and cook for 2 minutes.

3. Add garlic-onion-flour mixture to cooked meat. Then add remaining ingredients to meat mixture. Simmer for $1/2$ hour.

Yield: 9 servings
Serving size: 8 oz
Each serving provides:
Calories: 284
Total fat: 10 g
Saturated fat: 2 g
Cholesterol: 76 mg
Sodium: 162 mg
Total fiber: 4 g
Protein: 33 g
Carbohydrates: 16 g
Potassium: 769 mg

Beef Stroganoff

Lean top round beef and plain lowfat yogurt transform this rich dish into a heart healthy meal.

1 lb	lean beef (top round), cubed
2 tsp	vegetable oil
3/4 Tbsp	onion, finely chopped
1 lb	mushrooms, sliced
1/4 tsp	salt
to taste	pepper
1/4 tsp	nutmeg
1/2 tsp	dried basil
1/4 C	white wine
1 C	plain lowfat yogurt
6 C	macaroni, cooked in unsalted water

1. Cut beef into 1-inch cubes.

2. Heat 1 teaspoon oil in nonstick skillet. Sauté onion for 2 minutes.

3. Add beef and sauté for 5 minutes more. Turn to brown evenly. Remove from pan and keep hot.

4. Add remaining oil to pan and sauté mushrooms.

5. Add beef and onions to pan with seasonings.

6. Add wine and yogurt, and gently stir in. Heat, but do not boil.*

7. Serve with macaroni.

Yield: 5 servings
Serving size: 6 oz
Each serving provides:
Calories: 499
Total fat: 10 g
Saturated fat: 3 g
Cholesterol: 80 mg
Sodium: 200 mg
Total fiber: 4 g
Protein: 41 g
Carbohydrates: 58 g
Potassium: 891 mg

* If thickening is desired, use 2 teaspoons of cornstarch. Calories are same as for flour, but cornstarch has double the thickening power. The calories for cornstarch are not included in the nutrients per serving given above. To add cornstarch, take small amount of wine and yogurt broth and put aside to cool. Stir in cornstarch. Add some of warm broth to cornstarch paste and stir. Then, add cornstarch mixture to pan.

Black Skillet Beef With Greens and Red Potatoes

Here's a one-dish meal that tastes even better than it sounds.

1 lb	top round beef
1 Tbsp	paprika
1 1/2 tsp	oregano
1/2 tsp	chili powder
1/4 tsp	garlic powder
1/4 tsp	black pepper
1/8 tsp	red pepper
1/8 tsp	dry mustard
8	red-skinned potatoes, halved
3 C	onion, finely chopped
2 C	beef broth
2 cloves	large garlic, minced
2	large carrots, peeled, cut into very thin, 2 1/2-inch strips
2 bunch	(1/2 lb) mustard greens, kale, or turnip greens, stems removed, coarsely torn
as needed	nonstick cooking spray

Yield: 6 servings
Serving size: 7 oz
Each serving provides:
Calories: 340
Total fat: 5 g
Saturated fat: 2 g
Cholesterol: 64 mg
Sodium: 109 mg
Total fiber: 8 g
Protein: 30 g
Carbohydrates: 45 g
Potassium: 1,278 mg

1. Partially freeze beef. Thinly slice across grain into long strips 1/8-inch thick and 3 inches wide.

2. Combine paprika, oregano, chili powder, garlic powder, black pepper, red pepper, and dry mustard. Coat strips of meat with spice mixture.

3. Spray large, heavy skillet with nonstick coating. Preheat pan over high heat. Add meat and cook, stirring, for 5 minutes. Then add potatoes, onion, broth, and garlic, and cook covered over medium heat for 20 minutes. Stir in carrots, lay greens over top, and cook covered until carrots are tender, about 15 minutes.

4. Serve in large serving bowl with crusty bread for dunking.

Quick Beef Casserole

Tired? Busy? You don't need hours to make healthy dishes. Try this one-skillet wonder.

1/2 lb	lean ground beef
1 C	onion, chopped
1 C	celery, chopped
1 C	green pepper, cubed
3 1/2 C	tomatoes, diced
1/4 tsp	salt
1/2 tsp	black pepper
1/4 tsp	paprika
1 C	frozen peas
2	small carrots, diced
1 C	uncooked rice
1 1/2 C	water

1. In skillet, brown ground beef and drain off fat.

2. Add rest of ingredients. Mix well. Cover and cook over medium heat until boiling. Reduce to low heat and simmer for 35 minutes. Serve hot.

Yield: 8 servings
Serving size: 1 1/3 cups
Each serving provides:
Calories: 201
Total fat: 5 g
Saturated fat: 2 g
Cholesterol: 16 mg
Sodium: 164 mg
Total fiber: 3 g
Protein: 9 g
Carbohydrates: 31 g
Potassium: 449 mg

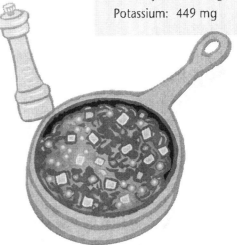

Scrumptious Meat Loaf

Got the meat loaf blahs? This recipe transforms the ordinary into the extraordinary.*

1 lb	ground beef, extra lean
1/2 C	(4 oz) tomato paste
1/4 C	onion, chopped
1/4 C	green peppers
1/4 C	red peppers
1 C	tomatoes, fresh, blanched, chopped
1/2 tsp	mustard, low sodium
1/4 tsp	ground black pepper
1/2 tsp	hot pepper, chopped
2 cloves	garlic, chopped
2 stalks	scallion, chopped
1/2 tsp	ground ginger
1/8 tsp	ground nutmeg
1 tsp	orange rind, grated
1/2 tsp	thyme, crushed
1/4 C	bread crumbs, finely grated

Yield: 6 servings
Serving size:
6, 1 1/4-inch-thick slices
Each serving provides:
Calories: 193
Total fat: 9 g
Saturated fat: 3 g
Cholesterol: 45 mg
Sodium: 91 mg
Total fiber: 2 g
Protein: 17 g
Carbohydrates: 11 g
Potassium: 513 mg

1. Mix all ingredients together.

2. Place in 1-pound loaf pan (preferably with drip rack) and bake covered at 350 °F for 50 minutes.

3. Uncover pan and continue baking for 12 minutes.

*For a different take on "meat loaf," try the turkey version on page 72.

Stir-Fried Beef and Potatoes

Vinegar and garlic give this easy-to-fix dish its tasty zip.

1 1/2 lb	sirloin steak
2 tsp	vegetable oil
1 clove	garlic, minced
1 tsp	vinegar
1/8 tsp	salt
1/8 tsp	pepper
2	large onions, sliced
1	large tomato, sliced
3 C	boiled potatoes, diced

1. Trim fat from steak and cut into small, thin pieces.

2. In large skillet, heat oil and sauté garlic until golden.

3. Add steak, vinegar, salt, and pepper. Cook for 6 minutes, stirring beef until brown.

4. Add onion and tomato. Cook until onion is transparent. Serve with boiled potatoes.

Yield: 6 servings
Serving size: 1 1/4 cup
Each serving provides:
Calories: 274
Total fat: 5 g
Saturated fat: 1 g
Cholesterol: 56 mg
Sodium: 96 mg
Total fiber: 3 g
Protein: 24 g
Carbohydrates: 33 g
Potassium: 878 mg

Stir-Fried Beef and Chinese Vegetables

2 Tbsp	dry red wine
1 Tbsp	soy sauce
$^1/_2$ tsp	sugar
$1^1/_2$ tsp	gingerroot, peeled, grated
1 lb	boneless round steak, fat trimmed, cut across grain into $1^1/_2$-inch strips
2 Tbsp	vegetable oil
2	medium onions, each cut into 8 wedges
$^1/_2$ lb	fresh mushrooms, rinsed, trimmed, sliced
2 stalks	($^1/_2$ C) celery, bias cut into $^1/_4$-inch slices
2	small green peppers, cut into thin lengthwise strips
1 C	water chestnuts, drained, sliced
2 Tbsp	cornstarch
$^1/_4$ C	water

Stir-frying uses very little oil, as this dish shows.

Yield: 6 servings
Serving size: 6 oz
Each serving provides:
Calories: 200
Total fat: 9 g
Saturated fat: 2 g
Cholesterol: 40 mg
Sodium: 201 mg
Total fiber: 3 g
Protein: 17 g
Carbohydrates: 12 g
Potassium: 552 mg

1. Prepare marinade by mixing together wine, soy sauce, sugar, and ginger.

2. Marinate meat in mixture while preparing vegetables.

3. Heat 1 tablespoon oil in large skillet or wok. Stir-fry onions and mushrooms for 3 minutes over medium-high heat.

4. Add celery and cook for 1 minute. Add remaining vegetables and cook for 2 minutes or until green pepper is tender but crisp. Transfer vegetables to warm bowl.

5. Add remaining 1 tablespoon oil to skillet. Stir-fry meat in oil for about 2 minutes, or until meat loses its pink color.

6. Blend cornstarch and water. Stir into meat. Cook and stir until thickened. Then return vegetables to skillet. Stir gently and serve.

Baked Pork Chops

You can really sink your chops into these—they're made spicy and moist with egg whites, evaporated milk, and a lively blend of herbs.

6	lean center-cut pork chops, $1/2$-inch thick*
1	egg white
1 C	evaporated skim milk
$3/4$ C	cornflake crumbs
$1/4$ C	fine dry bread crumbs
4 tsp	paprika
2 tsp	oregano
$3/4$ tsp	chili powder
$1/2$ tsp	garlic powder
$1/2$ tsp	black pepper
$1/8$ tsp	cayenne pepper
$1/8$ tsp	dry mustard
$1/2$ tsp	salt
as needed	nonstick cooking spray

*Try the recipe with skinless, boneless chicken or turkey parts, or fish—bake for just 20 minutes.

Yield: 6 servings
Serving size: 1 chop
Each serving provides:
Calories: 216
Total fat: 8 g
Saturated fat: 3 g
Cholesterol: 62 mg
Sodium: 346 mg
Total fiber: 1 g
Protein: 25 g
Carbohydrates: 10 g
Potassium: 414 mg

1. Preheat oven to 375 °F.

2. Trim fat from pork chops.

3. Beat egg white with evaporated skim milk. Place chops in milk mixture and let stand for 5 minutes, turning once.

4. Meanwhile, mix cornflake crumbs, bread crumbs, spices, and salt.

5. Use nonstick cooking spray on 13- by 9-inch baking pan.

6. Remove chops from milk mixture and coat thoroughly with crumb mixture.

7. Place chops in pan and bake at 375 °F for 20 minutes.
   Turn chops and bake for added 15 minutes or until no pink remains.

Shish Kabob

2 Tbsp	olive oil
1/2 C	chicken broth
1/4 C	red wine
1	lemon, juice only
1 tsp	chopped garlic
1/4 tsp	salt
1/2 tsp	rosemary
1/8 tsp	black pepper
2 lb	lean lamb, cut into 1-inch cubes
24	cherry tomatoes
24	mushrooms
24	small onions

The delicious taste of these kabobs comes from the lively marianade of wine, lemon juice, rosemary, and garlic.

1. Combine oil, broth, wine, lemon juice, garlic, salt, rosemary, and pepper. Pour over lamb, tomatoes, mushrooms, and onions. Marinate in refrigerator for several hours or overnight.

2. Put together skewers of lamb, onions, mushrooms, and tomatoes. Broil 3 inches from heat for 15 minutes, turning every 5 minutes.

Yield: 8 servings
Serving size: 1 kabob, with 3 oz of meat
Each serving provides:
Calories: 274
Total fat: 12 g
Saturated fat: 3 g
Cholesterol: 75 mg
Sodium: 207 mg
Total fiber: 3 g
Protein: 26 g
Carbohydrates: 16 g
Potassium: 728 mg

Spicy Veal Roast

Skimming the fat from the cooking juices in this dish helps lower the fat content.

1/4 tsp	salt
1/2 tsp	black pepper
1/2 tsp	cinnamon
1 1/2 tsp	cumin
3 lb	boned lean veal shoulder, trimmed, rolled, tied
4 tsp	olive oil
1/2 lb	onions, peeled
1/2 clove	garlic, peeled
2 tsp	dried tarragon
4 sprigs	fresh parsley
1 tsp	thyme
1	bay leaf

1. Mix together salt, pepper, cinnamon, and cumin. Rub over roast.

2. Heat 2 teaspoons of oil in large skillet. Add onions, garlic, and tarragon. Cover and cook over low heat for 10 minutes. Set aside.

3. Heat remaining 2 teaspoons of oil in ovenproof pan large enough to hold all ingredients. Brown meat on all sides.

4. Add garlic-onion mixture. Add parsley, thyme, and bay leaf. Cover.

5. Bake in 325 °F oven for 1 1/2 hours, or until meat is tender.

6. Remove meat to serving platter. Skim fat from cooking juices. Remove bay leaf and parsley. Cut roast in 1/4- to 1/2-inch slices. Pour a little cooking juice over roast and serve rest on side.

Yield: 12 servings
Serving size: 3 oz
Each serving provides:
Calories: 206
Total fat: 8 g
Saturated fat: 3 g
Cholesterol: 124 mg
Sodium: 149 mg
Total fiber: 1 g
Protein: 30 g
Carbohydrates: 2 g
Potassium: 459 mg

Barbecued Chicken

Don't forget to remove the skin and fat to keep this zesty dish heart healthy.

3 lb	chicken parts (breast, drumstick, and thigh), skin and fat removed
1	large onion, thinly sliced
3 Tbsp	vinegar
3 Tbsp	Worcestershire sauce
2 Tbsp	brown sugar
to taste	black pepper
1 Tbsp	hot pepper flakes
1 Tbsp	chili powder
1 C	chicken stock or broth, fat skimmed from top

1. Place chicken in 13- by 9- by 2-inch pan. Arrange onions over top.

2. Mix together vinegar, Worcestershire sauce, brown sugar, pepper, hot pepper flakes, chili powder, and stock.

3. Pour mixture over chicken and bake at 350 °F for 1 hour or until done. While cooking, baste occasionally.

Yield: 8 servings
Serving size: 1 chicken part with sauce
Each serving provides:
Calories: 176
Total fat: 6 g
Saturated fat: 2 g
Cholesterol: 68 mg
Sodium: 240 mg
Total fiber: 1 g
Protein: 24 g
Carbohydrates: 7 g
Potassium: 360 mg

Barbecued Chicken–Spicy Southern Style

Let yourself fall under the spell of this Southern-style, sweet, barbecue sauce.

5 Tbsp	(3 oz) tomato paste
1 tsp	ketchup
2 tsp	honey
1 tsp	molasses
1 tsp	Worcestershire sauce
4 tsp	white vinegar
$3/4$ tsp	cayenne pepper
$1/8$ tsp	black pepper
$1/4$ tsp	onion powder
2 cloves	garlic, minced
$1/8$ tsp	ginger, grated
$1^1/2$ lb	chicken (breasts, drumsticks), skinless

1. Combine all ingredients except chicken in saucepan.

2. Simmer for 15 minutes.

3. Wash chicken and pat dry. Place it on large platter and brush with half of sauce mixture.

4. Cover with plastic wrap and marinate in refrigerator for 1 hour.

5. Place chicken on baking sheet lined with aluminum foil and broil for 10 minutes on each side to seal in juices.

6. Turn oven to 350 °F and add remaining sauce to chicken. Cover chicken with aluminum foil and continue baking for 30 minutes.

Yield: 6 servings
Serving size: $1/2$ breast or 2 small drumsticks
Each serving provides:
Calories: 176
Total fat: 4 g
Saturated fat: less than 1 g
Cholesterol: 81 mg
Sodium: 199 mg
Total fiber: 1 g
Protein: 27 g
Carbohydrates: 7 g
Potassium: 392 mg

Chicken Gumbo

Simple but filling—
this dish feeds
the need.

1 tsp	vegetable oil
$1/4$ C	flour
3 C	low-sodium chicken broth
1 $1/2$ lb	chicken breast, skinless, boneless, cut into 1-inch strips
1 C	($1/2$ lb) white potatoes, cubed
1 C	onions, chopped
1 C	($1/2$ lb) carrots, coarsely chopped
$1/2$	medium carrot, grated
$1/4$ C	celery, chopped
4 cloves	garlic, finely minced
2 stalks	scallion, chopped
1	whole bay leaf
$1/2$ tsp	thyme
$1/2$ tsp	black pepper, ground
2 tsp	hot (or jalapeño) pepper
1 C	($1/2$ lb) okra, sliced into $1/2$-inch pieces

Yield: 8 servings
Serving size: $3/4$ cup
Each serving provides:
Calories: 165
Total fat: 4 g
Saturated fat: 1 g
Cholesterol: 51 mg
Sodium: 81 mg
Total fiber: 2 g
Protein: 21 g
Carbohydrates: 11 g
Potassium: 349 mg

1. Add oil to large pot and heat over medium flame.

2. Stir in flour. Cook, stirring constantly, until flour begins to turn golden brown.

3. Slowly stir in all broth using wire whisk. Cook for 2 minutes. Broth mixture should not be lumpy.

4. Add rest of ingredients except okra. Bring to boil, then reduce heat and let simmer for 20–30 minutes.

5. Add okra and let cook for 15–20 more minutes.

6. Remove bay leaf and serve hot in bowl or over rice.

Chicken and Rice

Let this Latino-inspired dish—full of heart healthy ingredients—inspire you.

6	chicken pieces (legs and breasts), skinless
2 tsp	vegetable oil
4 C	water
2	tomatoes, chopped
$1/2$ C	green pepper, chopped
$1/4$ C	red pepper, chopped
$1/4$ C	celery, diced
1	medium carrot, grated
$1/4$ C	corn, frozen
$1/2$ C	onion, chopped
$1/4$ C	fresh cilantro, chopped
2 cloves	garlic, chopped fine
$1/8$ tsp	salt
$1/8$ tsp	pepper
2 C	rice
$1/2$ C	frozen peas
2 oz	Spanish olives
$1/4$ C	raisins

Yield: 6 servings
Serving size: 1 cup of rice and 1 piece of chicken
Each serving provides:
Calories: 448
Total fat: 7 g
Saturated fat: 2 g
Cholesterol: 49 mg
Sodium: 352 mg
Total fiber: 4 g
Protein: 24 g
Carbohydrates: 70 g
Potassium: 551 mg

1. In large pot, brown chicken pieces in oil.

2. Add water, tomatoes, green and red peppers, celery, carrots, corn, onion, cilantro, garlic, salt, and pepper. Cover and cook over medium heat for 20–30 minutes or until chicken is done.

3. Remove chicken from pot and place in refrigerator. Add rice, peas, and olives to pot. Cover pot and cook over low heat for about 20 minutes until rice is done.

4. Add chicken and raisins, and cook for another 8 minutes.

Chicken and Spanish Rice

This peppy dish is moderate in sodium but high in taste.

1 C	onions, chopped
1/4 C	green peppers
2 tsp	vegetable oil
1 can	(8 oz) tomato sauce*
1 tsp	parsley, chopped
1/2 tsp	black pepper
1 1/4 tsp	garlic, minced
5 C	cooked rice (in unsalted water)
3 1/2 C	chicken breast, cooked, skin and bone removed, diced

*Reduce sodium by using one 4-oz can of no salt added tomato sauce and one 4-oz can of regular tomato sauce. New sodium content for each serving is 226 mg.

1. In large skillet, sauté onions and green peppers in oil for 5 minutes on medium heat.
2. Add tomato sauce and spices. Heat through.
3. Add cooked rice and chicken, and heat through.

Yield: 5 servings
Serving size: 1 1/2 cups
Each serving provides:
Calories: 406
Total fat: 6 g
Saturated fat: 2 g
Cholesterol: 75 mg
Sodium: 367 mg
Total fiber: 2 g
Protein: 33 g
Carbohydrates: 52 g
Potassium: 527 mg

Chicken Marsala

Want flavor without lots of salt and fat? Try this dish, which combines wine, lemon juice, and mushrooms into a delicious sauce.

1/8 tsp	black pepper
1/4 tsp	salt
1/4 C	flour
4	(5 oz total) chicken breasts, boned, skinless
1 Tbsp	olive oil
1/2 C	Marsala wine
1/2 C	chicken stock, fat skimmed from top
1/2	lemon, juice only
1/2 C	mushrooms, sliced
1 Tbsp	fresh parsley, chopped

1. Mix together pepper, salt, and flour. Coat chicken with seasoned flour.

2. In heavy-bottomed skillet, heat oil. Place chicken breasts in skillet and brown on both sides, then remove and set aside.

3. To skillet, add wine and stir until heated. Add juice, stock, and mushrooms. Stir, reduce heat, and cook for about 10 minutes, until sauce is partially reduced.

4. Return browned chicken breasts to skillet. Spoon sauce over chicken.

5. Cover and cook for about 5–10 minutes or until chicken is done.

6. Serve sauce over chicken. Garnish with chopped parsley.

Yield: 4 servings
Serving size: 1 chicken breast with 1/3 cup of sauce
Each serving provides:
Calories: 285
Total fat: 8 g
Saturated fat: 2 g
Cholesterol: 85 mg
Sodium: 236 mg
Total fiber: 1 g
Protein: 33 g
Carbohydrates: 11 g
Potassium: 348 mg

Chicken Orientale

Kabobs look as great as they taste, and these are made with no added salt and very little oil, in order to keep them heart healthy.

8	boneless, skinless chicken breasts, cut into chunks
8	fresh mushrooms
to taste	black pepper
8	whole white onions, parboiled
2	oranges, quartered
8	canned pineapple chunks, nonsweetened
8	cherry tomatoes
1 can	(6 oz) frozen, concentrated apple juice, thawed
1 C	dry white wine
2 Tbsp	soy sauce, low sodium
dash	ginger, ground
2 Tbsp	vinegar
1/4 C	vegetable oil

1. Sprinkle chicken breasts with pepper.

2. Thread 8 skewers as follows: chicken, mushroom, chicken, onion, chicken, orange quarter, chicken, pineapple chunk, cherry tomato. Place kabobs in shallow pan.

3. Combine remaining ingredients and spoon over kabobs. Marinate in refrigerator for at least 1 hour, then drain.

4. Broil kabobs 6 inches from heat for 15 minutes for each side. Brush with marinade every 5 minutes. After done, discard leftover marinade and serve kabobs.

Yield: 8 servings
Serving size: 1/2 kabob
Each serving provides:
Calories: 359
Total fat: 11 g
Saturated fat: 2 g
Cholesterol: 66 mg
Sodium: 226 mg
Total fiber: 3 g
Protein: 28 g
Carbohydrates: 34 g
Potassium: 756 mg

Chicken Ratatouille

It may be hard to say ratatouille, but this one-dish recipe will show you that it's very easy to eat.

1 Tbsp	vegetable oil
4	medium chicken breast halves, skinned, fat removed, boned, and cut into 1-inch pieces
2	zucchini, about 7 inches long, unpeeled, thinly sliced
1	small eggplant, peeled, cut into 1-inch cubes
1	medium onion, thinly sliced
1	medium green pepper, cut into 1-inch pieces
$1/2$ lb	fresh mushrooms, sliced
1 can	(16 oz) whole tomatoes, cut up
1 clove	garlic, minced
1 $1/2$ tsp	dried basil, crushed
1 Tbsp	fresh parsley, minced
to taste	black pepper

1. Heat oil in large nonstick skillet. Add chicken and sauté for about 3 minutes or until lightly browned.

2. Add zucchini, eggplant, onion, green pepper, and mushrooms. Cook for about 15 minutes, stirring occasionally.

3. Add tomatoes, garlic, basil, parsley, and pepper. Stir and continue to cook for about 5 minutes or until chicken is tender.

Yield: 4 servings
Serving size: 1$1/2$ cups
Each serving provides:
Calories: 266
Total fat: 8 g
Saturated fat: 2 g
Cholesterol: 66 mg
Sodium: 253 mg
Total fiber: 6 g
Protein: 30 g
Carbohydrates: 21 g
Potassium: 1,148 mg

Chicken Salad

Chill out
with this simple,
yet flavorful dish.

3 1/4 C	chicken, cooked, cubed, skinless
1/4 C	celery, chopped
1 Tbsp	lemon juice
1/2 tsp	onion powder
1/8 tsp	salt*
3 Tbsp	mayonnaise, lowfat

*Reduce sodium by removing the 1/8 tsp of added salt. New sodium content for each serving is 127 mg.

1. Bake chicken, cut into cubes, and refrigerate.
2. In large bowl, combine rest of ingredients, add chilled chicken and mix well.

Yield: 5 servings
Serving size: 3/4 cup
Each serving provides:
Calories: 183
Total fat: 7 g
Saturated fat: 2 g
Cholesterol: 78 mg
Sodium: 201 mg
Total fiber: 0 g
Protein: 27 g
Carbohydrates: 1 g
Potassium: 240 mg

Chicken Stew

This stew is as hearty as any, but healthier than most.

8 pieces	chicken (breasts or legs)
1 C	water
2 cloves	small garlic, minced
1	small onion, chopped
1 $^1/_2$ tsp	salt
$^1/_2$ tsp	pepper
3	medium tomatoes, chopped
1 tsp	parsley, chopped
$^1/_4$ C	celery, finely chopped
2	medium potatoes, peeled, chopped
2	small carrots, chopped
2	bay leaves

1. Remove skin from chicken, along with any extra fat. In large skillet, combine chicken, water, garlic, onion, salt, pepper, tomatoes, and parsley. Tightly cover and cook over low heat for 25 minutes.

2. Add celery, potatoes, carrots, and bay leaves and continue to cook for 15 more minutes or until chicken and vegetables are tender. Remove bay leaves before serving.

Yield: 8 servings
Serving size: 1 piece of chicken
Each serving provides:
Calories: 206
Total fat: 6 g
Saturated fat: 2 g
Cholesterol: 75 mg
Sodium: 489 mg
Total fiber: 2 g
Protein: 28 g
Carbohydrates: 10 g
Potassium: 493 mg

Crispy Oven-Fried Chicken

Kids will love this chicken—it tastes batter-dipped and fried, but is actually good for the heart.

$1/2$ C	skim milk or buttermilk
1 tsp	poultry seasoning
1 C	cornflakes, crumbled
1 $1/2$ Tbsp	onion powder
1 $1/2$ Tbsp	garlic powder
2 tsp	black pepper
2 tsp	dried hot pepper, crushed
1 tsp	ginger, ground
8 pieces	chicken, skinless (4 breasts, 4 drumsticks)
a few	shakes of paprika
1 tsp	vegetable oil

1. Preheat oven to 350 °F.

2. Add $1/2$ teaspoon of poultry seasoning to milk.

3. Combine all other spices with corn-flake crumbs and place in plastic bag.

4. Wash chicken and pat dry. Dip chicken into milk, shake to remove excess, then quickly shake in bag with seasoning and crumbs.

5. Refrigerate for 1 hour.

6. Remove from refrigerator and sprinkle lightly with paprika for color.

7. Evenly space chicken on greased baking pan.

8. Cover with aluminum foil and bake for 40 minutes. Remove foil and continue baking for an added 30–40 minutes or until meat can be easily pulled away from bone with fork. Drumsticks may require less baking time than breasts. (Do not turn chicken during baking.) Crumbs will form crispy "skin."

Yield: 6 servings
Serving size: $1/2$ breast or 2 small drumsticks
Each serving provides:
Calories: 256
Total fat: 5 g
Saturated fat: 1 g
Cholesterol: 82 mg
Sodium: 286 mg
Total fiber: 1 g
Protein: 30 g
Carbohydrates: 22 g
Potassium: 339 mg

Finger-Licking Curried Chicken

The name tells all— ginger and curry powder make this dish irresistible.

1 1/2 tsp	curry powder
1 tsp	thyme, crushed
1 stalk	scallion, chopped
1 Tbsp	hot pepper, chopped
1 tsp	black pepper, ground
8 cloves	garlic, crushed
1 Tbsp	ginger, grated
3/4 tsp	salt
8 pieces	chicken, skinless (breast and drumstick)
1 Tbsp	olive oil
1 C	water
1	medium white potato, diced
1	large onion, chopped

1. Mix together curry powder, thyme, scallion, hot pepper, cayenne pepper, black pepper, garlic, ginger, onion, and salt.

2. Sprinkle seasoning mixture on chicken.

3. Marinate for at least 2 hours in refrigerator.

4. Heat oil in skillet over medium flame. Add chicken and sauté.

5. Add water and allow chicken to cook over medium flame for 30 minutes.

6. Add diced potatoes and cook for an added 30 minutes.

7. Add onions and cook for 15 minutes more or until meat is tender.

Yield: 6 servings
Serving size: 1/2 breast or 2 small drumsticks
Each serving provides:
Calories: 213
Total fat: 6 g
Saturated fat: 2 g
Cholesterol: 81 mg
Sodium: 363 mg
Total fiber: 1 g
Protein: 28 g
Carbohydrates: 10 g
Potassium: 384 mg

Grilled Chicken With Green Chile Sauce

In this recipe, the chicken is marinated to make it tender without using a lot of fat.

4	chicken breasts, boneless, skinless
1/4 C	olive oil
2	limes, juice only
1/4 tsp	oregano
1/2 tsp	black pepper
1/4 C	water
10–12	tomatillos, husks removed, cut in half
1/2	medium onion, quartered
2 cloves	garlic, finely chopped
2	jalapeño peppers
2 Tbsp	cilantro, chopped
1/4 tsp	salt
1/4 C	lowfat sour cream

Yield: 4 servings
Serving size: 1 breast
Each serving provides:
Calories: 210
Total fat: 5 g
Saturated fat: 1 g
Cholesterol: 73 mg
Sodium: 91 mg
Total fiber: 3 g
Protein: 29 g
Carbohydrates: 14 g
Potassium: 780 mg

1. Combine oil, juice from one lime, oregano, and black pepper in shallow, glass baking dish. Stir.

2. Place chicken breasts in baking dish and turn to coat each side. Cover dish and refrigerate overnight. Turn chicken periodically to marinate it on both sides.

3. Put water, tomatillos, and onion into saucepan. Bring to gentle boil and cook uncovered for 10 minutes or until tomatillos are tender.

4. In blender, place cooked onion, tomatillos, and any remaining water. Add garlic, jalapeño peppers, cilantro, salt, and juice of second lime. Blend until all ingredients are smooth. Place sauce in bowl and refrigerate.

5. Place chicken breasts on hot grill and cook until done. Place chicken on serving platter. Spoon tablespoon of lowfat sour cream over each chicken breast. Pour sauce over sour cream.

Jamaican Jerk Chicken

The spices and peppers in this dish will transport you to a whole new taste.

$1/2$ tsp	cinnamon, ground
$1^1/2$ tsp	allspice, ground
$1^1/2$ tsp	black pepper, ground
1 Tbsp	hot pepper, chopped
1 tsp	hot pepper, crushed, dried
2 tsp	oregano, crushed
2 tsp	thyme, crushed
$1/2$ tsp	salt
6 cloves	garlic, finely chopped
1 C	onion, pureed or finely chopped
$1/4$ C	vinegar
3 Tbsp	brown sugar
8 pieces	chicken, skinless (4 breasts, 4 drumsticks)

1. Preheat oven to 350 °F.

2. Combine all ingredients except chicken in large bowl. Rub seasoning over chicken and marinate in refrigerator for 6 hours or longer.

3. Evenly space chicken on nonstick or lightly greased baking pan.

4. Cover with aluminum foil and bake for 40 minutes. Remove foil and continue baking for an added 30–40 minutes or until the meat can be easily pulled away from the bone with a fork.

Yields: 6 servings
Serving size: $1/2$ breast or 2 small drumsticks
Each serving provides:
Calories: 199
Total fat: 4 g
Saturated fat: 1 g
Cholesterol: 81 mg
Sodium: 267 mg
Total fiber: 1 g
Protein: 28 g
Carbohydrates: 12 g
Potassium: 338 mg

20-Minute Chicken Creole

This quick Southern dish contains no added fat and very little added salt in its spicy tomato sauce.

4	medium chicken breast halves, skinless, boned, and cut into 1-inch strips*
1 C	(14 oz) tomatoes, cut up**
1 C	low-sodium chili sauce
1¹/₂ C	(1 large) green pepper, chopped
1¹/₂ C	celery, chopped
¹/₄ C	onion, chopped
2 cloves	garlic, minced
1 Tbsp	fresh basil (or 1 tsp dried)
1 Tbsp	fresh parsley (or 1 tsp dried)
¹/₄ tsp	red pepper, crushed
¹/₄ tsp	salt
as needed	nonstick cooking spray

* For convenience, you can use uncooked boneless, skinless chicken breast.

** To cut back on sodium, try low sodium canned tomatoes.

1. Spray deep skillet with nonstick cooking spray. Preheat pan over high heat.

2. Cook chicken in hot skillet, stirring, for 3–5 minutes or until no longer pink. Reduce heat.

3. Add tomatoes with juice, low sodium chili sauce, green pepper, celery, onion, garlic, basil, parsley, crushed red pepper, and salt. Bring to boil and reduce heat. Simmer covered for 10 minutes.

4. Serve over hot cooked rice or whole wheat pasta.

Yield: 4 servings
Serving size: 1¹/₂ cups
Each serving provides:
Calories: 274
Total fat: 5 g
Saturated fat: 1 g
Cholesterol: 73 mg
Sodium: 383 mg
Total fiber: 4 g
Protein: 30 g
Carbohydrates: 30 g
Potassium: 944 mg

Very Lemony Chicken

This tangy chicken scores high on taste, while being lower in calories, saturated fat, and cholesterol.

1 ¹/₂ lb	chicken breast, skinned, fat removed
¹/₂ C	fresh lemon juice
2 Tbsp	white wine vinegar
¹/₂ C	fresh lemon peel, sliced
3 tsp	fresh oregano, chopped (or 1 tsp dried oregano, crushed)
1	medium onion, sliced
¹/₄ tsp	salt
to taste	black pepper
¹/₂ tsp	paprika

1. Place chicken in 13- by 9- by 2-inch glass baking dish.

2. Mix lemon juice, vinegar, lemon peel, oregano, and onions. Pour over chicken, cover, and marinate in refrigerator several hours, turning occasionally, or overnight.

3. Sprinkle with salt, pepper, and paprika.

4. Cover and bake at 300 °F for 30 minutes. Uncover and bake for added 30 minutes or until done.

Yield: 4 servings
Serving size:
1 breast with sauce
Each serving provides:
Calories: 179
Total fat: 4 g
Saturated fat: 1 g
Cholesterol: 73 mg
Sodium: 222 mg
Total fiber: 2 g
Protein: 28 g
Carbohydrates: 8 g
Potassium: 350 mg

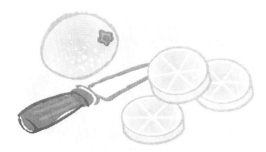

Yosemite Chicken Stew and Dumplings

This satisfying dish keeps the fat down so you can enjoy its dumplings without turning into one.

FOR STEW

1 lb	chicken, skinless, boneless, cut into 1-inch cubes
$1/2$ C	onion, coarsely chopped
1	medium carrot, peeled, thinly sliced
1 stalk	celery, thinly sliced
$1/4$ tsp	salt
to taste	black pepper
1 pinch	ground cloves
1	bay leaf
3 C	water
1 tsp	cornstarch
1 tsp	dried basil
1 package	(10 oz) frozen peas

FOR CORNMEAL DUMPLINGS

1 C	yellow cornmeal
$3/4$ C	sifted all-purpose flour
2 tsp	baking powder
$1/2$ tsp	salt
1 C	lowfat milk
1 Tbsp	vegetable oil

Yield: 6 servings
Serving size: 1$1/4$ cups stew with 2 dumplings
Each serving provides:
Calories: 301
Total fat: 6 g
Saturated fat: 1 g
Cholesterol: 43 mg
Sodium: 471 mg
Total fiber: 5 g
Protein: 24 g
Carbohydrates: 37 g
Potassium: 409 mg

To prepare stew:

1. Place chicken, onion, carrot, celery, salt, pepper, cloves, bay leaf, and water in large saucepan. Heat to boiling. Cover and reduce heat to simmer. Cook for about 30 minutes or until chicken is tender.

2. Remove chicken and vegetables from broth. Strain broth.

continued on next page

67

Yosemite Chicken Stew and Dumplings *(continued)*

3. Skim fat from broth. Measure and, if necessary, add water to make 3 cups liquid.

4. Add cornstarch to 1 cup of cooled broth and mix by shaking vigorously in jar with tight-fitting lid.

5. Pour mix into saucepan with remaining broth. Cook, stirring constantly, until liquid comes to boil and is thickened.

6. Add basil, peas, and reserved vegetables to sauce. Stir to combine.

7. Add chicken and heat slowly to boiling while preparing cornmeal dumplings.

To prepare dumplings:

1. Put cornmeal, flour, baking powder, and salt into large mixing bowl.

2. Mix milk and oil. Add milk mixture all at once to dry ingredients. Stir just enough to moisten flour and evenly distribute liquid. Dough will be soft.

3. Drop by full tablespoons on top of stew. Cover saucepan tightly. Heat to boiling. Reduce heat to simmering, and steam for about 20 minutes. Do not lift cover.

Autumn Turkey-Stuffed Cabbage

This dish cuts the fat by mixing turkey and lean beef.

1 head	cabbage
$1/2$ lb	lean ground beef
$1/2$ lb	ground turkey
2	small onions, one minced, one sliced
1 slice	stale whole wheat bread, crumbled
$1/4$ C	water
$1/8$ tsp	black pepper
1 can	(16 oz) diced tomatoes
1 C	water
1	medium carrot, sliced
1 Tbsp	lemon juice
2 Tbsp	brown sugar
1 Tbsp	cornstarch

1. Rinse and core cabbage. Carefully remove 10 outer leaves and place in saucepan. Cover with boiling water and simmer for 5 minutes. Remove cooked cabbage leaves and drain on paper towel.

2. Shred $1/2$ cup of raw cabbage and set aside.

3. Brown ground beef and turkey, and minced onion in skillet. Drain fat.

4. Place cooked and drained meat mixture, bread crumbs, water, and pepper in mixing bowl.

Yield: 5 servings
Serving size: 2 rolls
Each serving provides:
Calories: 235
Total fat: 9 g
Saturated fat: 3 g
Cholesterol: 56 mg
Sodium: 235 mg
Total fiber: 3 g
Protein: 20 g
Carbohydrates: 18 g
Potassium: 545 mg

continued on next page

Autumn Turkey-Stuffed Cabbage *(continued)*

5. Drain tomatoes, reserving liquid, and add $1/2$ cup tomato juice from can to meat mixture. Mix well. Place $1/4$ cup of filling on each parboiled, drained cabbage leaf. Fold. Place folded side down in skillet.

6. Add tomatoes, sliced onion, water, shredded cabbage, and carrot. Cover and simmer for about 1 hour or until cabbage is tender, basting occasionally.

7. Remove cabbage rolls to serving platter, keep warm.

8. Mix lemon juice, brown sugar, and cornstarch together in small bowl. Add to vegetables and liquid in skillet and cook, stirring occasionally, until thickened and clear.
Serve over cabbage rolls.

Spaghetti With Turkey Meat Sauce

Turkey isn't just for Thanksgiving. Let it go Italian for this healthy, meaty spaghetti.

1 lb	ground turkey, lean
1 can	(28 oz) tomatoes, cut up
1 C	green pepper, finely chopped
1 C	onion, finely chopped
2 cloves	garlic, minced
1 tsp	dried oregano, crushed
1 tsp	black pepper
1 lb	spaghetti, uncooked
as needed	nonstick cooking spray

1. Coat large skillet with nonstick spray. Preheat over high heat.

2. Add turkey and cook, stirring occasionally, for 5 minutes. Drain and discard fat.

3. Stir in tomatoes with juice, green pepper, onion, garlic, oregano, and black pepper. Bring to boil. Reduce heat and simmer covered for 15 minutes, stirring occasionally. Remove cover and simmer for added 15 minutes. (For creamier sauce, give sauce a whirl in blender or food processor.)

4. Meanwhile, cook spaghetti in unsalted water. Drain well.

5. Serve sauce over spaghetti.

Yield: 6 servings
Serving size:
5 oz of sauce with
9 oz of cooked spaghetti
Each serving provides:
Calories: 455
Total fat: 6 g
Saturated fat: 1 g
Cholesterol: 51 mg
Sodium: 248 mg
Total fiber: 5 g
Protein: 28 g
Carbohydrates: 71 g
Potassium: 593 mg

Turkey Meat Loaf

Here's a healthier version of an old diner favorite.

1 lb	lean turkey, ground
1/2 C	regular oats, dry
1	large egg
1 Tbsp	onion, dehydrated
1/4 C	catsup

1. Combine all ingredients and mix well.
2. Bake in loaf pan at 350 °F or to internal temperature of 165 °F for 25 minutes.
3. Cut into five slices and serve.

Yield: 5 servings
Serving size: 1 slice (3 oz)
Each serving yields:
Calories: 192
Total fat: 7 g
Saturated fat: 2 g
Cholesterol: 103 mg
Sodium: 214 mg
Total fiber: 1 g
Protein: 21 g
Carbohydrates: 23 g
Potassium: 292 mg

Baked Salmon Dijon

This salmon entrée is easy to make and will be enjoyed by the whole family!

1 C	fat free sour cream
2 tsp	dried dill
3 Tbsp	scallions, finely chopped
2 Tbsp	Dijon mustard
2 Tbsp	lemon juice
1 1/2 lb	salmon fillet with skin, cut in center
1/2 tsp	garlic powder
1/2 tsp	black pepper
as needed	fat free cooking spray

1. Whisk sour cream, dill, onion, mustard, and lemon juice in small bowl to blend.

2. Preheat oven to 400 °F. Lightly oil baking sheet with cooking spray.

3. Place salmon, skin side down, on prepared sheet. Sprinkle with garlic powder and pepper, then spread with the sauce.

4. Bake salmon until just opaque in center, about 20 minutes.

Yield: 6 servings
Serving size:
1 piece (4 oz)
Each serving provides:
Calories: 196
Total fat: 7 g
Saturated fat: 2 g
Cholesterol: 76 mg
Sodium: 229 mg
Total fiber: less than 1 g
Protein: 27 g
Carbohydrates: 5 g
Potassium: 703 mg

Baked Trout

You'll reel them in with this nutritious delicious dish.

2 lb	trout fillet, cut into 6 pieces Any kind of fish can be used.
3 Tbsp	lime juice (about 2 limes)
1	medium tomato, chopped
1/2	medium onion, chopped
3 Tbsp	cilantro, chopped
1/2 tsp	olive oil
1/4 tsp	black pepper
1/4 tsp	salt
1/4 tsp	red pepper (optional)

1. Preheat oven to 350 °F.

2. Rinse fish and pat dry. Place in baking dish.

3. In separate dish, mix remaining ingredients together and pour over fish.

4. Bake for 15–20 minutes or until fork-tender.

Yield: 6 servings
Serving size: 1 piece
Each serving provides:
Calories: 236
Total fat: 9 g
Saturated fat: 3 g
Cholesterol: 104 mg
Sodium: 197 mg
Total fiber: less than 1 g
Protein: 34 g
Carbohydrates: 2 g
Potassium: 865 mg

Catfish Stew and Rice

Catfish isn't just Southern anymore. Everyone can go "down home" with this dish.

2	medium potatoes
1 can	(14$^1/_2$ oz) tomatoes, cut up*
1 C	onion, chopped
1 C	(8–oz bottle) clam juice or water
1 C	water
2 cloves	garlic, minced
$^1/_2$ head	cabbage, coarsely chopped
1 lb	catfish fillets
as needed	green onion, sliced
1$^1/_2$ Tbsp	Chili and Spice Seasoning (see page 138)
2 C	cooked rice (white or brown)

* Reduce the sodium by using low or no added sodium canned tomatoes.

1. Peel potatoes and cut into quarters.

2. In large pot, combine potatoes, tomatoes and their juice, onion, clam juice, water, and garlic. Bring to boil and reduce heat. Cook covered over medium-low heat for 10 minutes.

3. Add cabbage and return to boil. Reduce heat. Cook covered over medium-low heat for 5 minutes, stirring occasionally.

4. Meanwhile, cut fillets into 2-inch lengths. Coat with Chili and Spice Seasoning.

5. Add fish to vegetables. Reduce heat and simmer covered for 5 minutes or until fish flakes easily with fork.

6. Serve in soup plates. Garnish with sliced green onion, if desired. Serve with scoop of hot cooked rice.

Yield: 4 servings
Serving size: 1 cup of stew with $^1/_2$ cup of rice
Each serving provides:
Calories: 363
Total fat: 8 g
Saturated fat: 2 g
Cholesterol: 87 mg
Sodium: 355 mg
Total fiber: 4 g
Protein: 28 g
Carbohydrates: 44 g
Potassium: 1,079 mg

Fish Veronique

1 lb	white fish (such as cod, sole, or turbot)
$1/4$ tsp	salt
$1/8$ tsp	black pepper
$1/4$ C	dry white wine
$1/4$ C	chicken stock or broth, skim fat from top
1 Tbsp	lemon juice
1 Tbsp	soft margarine
2 Tbsp	flour
$3/4$ C	lowfat or skim milk
$1/2$ C	seedless grapes
as needed	nonstick cooking spray

Here's a trick to treat the taste buds: Remove the fat from the chicken broth and add lowfat milk to get a healthy sauce that tastes rich and looks creamy.

1. Spray 10- by 6-inch baking dish with nonstick spray. Place fish in pan and sprinkle with salt and pepper.

2. Mix wine, stock, and lemon juice in small bowl and pour over fish.

3. Cover and bake at 350 °F for 15 minutes.

4. Melt margarine in small saucepan. Remove from heat and blend in flour. Gradually add milk and cook over moderately low heat, stirring constantly, until thickened.

5. Remove fish from oven, and pour liquid from baking dish into "cream" sauce, stirring until blended. Pour sauce over fish and sprinkle with grapes.

6. Broil about 4 inches from heat for 5 minutes or until sauce starts to brown.

Yield: 4 servings
Serving size: 1 fillet with sauce
Each serving provides:
Calories: 166
Total fat: 2 g
Saturated fat: 1 g
Cholesterol: 61 mg
Sodium: 343 mg
Total fiber: less than 1 g
Protein: 24 g
Carbohydrates: 9 g
Potassium: 453 mg

Mediterranean Baked Fish

Taste the Mediterranean in this dish's tomato, onion, and garlic sauce.

1 lb	fish fillets (sole, flounder, or sea perch)
2 tsp	olive oil
1	large onion, sliced
1 can	(16 oz) whole tomatoes, drained (reserve juice), coarsely chopped
$1/2$ C	tomato juice (reserved from canned tomatoes)
1	bay leaf
1 clove	garlic, minced
1 C	dry white wine
$1/4$ C	lemon juice
$1/4$ C	orange juice
1 Tbsp	fresh orange peel, grated
1 tsp	fennel seeds, crushed
$1/2$ tsp	dried oregano, crushed
$1/2$ tsp	dried thyme, crushed
$1/2$ tsp	dried basil, crushed
to taste	black pepper

Yield: 4 servings
Serving size:
4-oz fillet with sauce
Each serving provides:
Calories: 178
Total fat: 4 g
Saturated fat: 1 g
Cholesterol: 56 mg
Sodium: 260 mg
Total fiber: 3 g
Protein: 22 g
Carbohydrates: 12 g
Potassium: 678 mg

1. Heat oil in large nonstick skillet. Add onion and sauté over moderate heat for 5 minutes or until soft.

2. Add all remaining ingredients except fish. Stir well and simmer uncovered for 30 minutes.

3. Arrange fish in 10- by 6-inch baking dish. Cover with sauce. Bake uncovered at 375 °F for about 15 minutes or until fish flakes easily.

Mouth-Watering Oven-Fried Fish

This heart healthy dish can be made with many kinds of fish—to be enjoyed over and over.

2 lb	fish fillets
1 Tbsp	lemon juice, fresh
1/4 C	skim milk or 1% buttermilk
2 drops	hot pepper sauce
1 tsp	fresh garlic, minced
1/4 tsp	white pepper, ground
1/4 tsp	salt
1/4 tsp	onion powder
1/2 C	cornflakes, crumbled, or regular bread crumbs
1 Tbsp	vegetable oil
1	fresh lemon, cut in wedges

1. Preheat oven to 475 °F.

2. Wipe fillets with lemon juice and pat dry.

3. Combine milk, hot pepper sauce, and garlic.

4. Combine pepper, salt, and onion powder with cornflake crumbs and place on plate.

5. Let fillets sit briefly in milk. Remove and coat fillets on both sides with seasoned crumbs. Let stand briefly until coating sticks to each side of fish.

6. Arrange on lightly oiled shallow baking dish.

7. Bake for 20 minutes on middle rack without turning.

8. Cut into 6 pieces. Serve with fresh lemon.

Yield: 6 servings
Serving size: 1 cut piece
Each serving provides:
Calories: 183
Total fat: 2 g
Saturated fat: less than 1 g
Cholesterol: 80 mg
Sodium: 325 mg
Total fiber: 1 g
Protein: 30 g
Carbohydrates: 10 g
Potassium: 453 mg

Scallop Kabobs

These colorful kabobs use scallops, which are naturally low in saturated fat.

3	medium green peppers, cut into 1$1/2$-inch squares
1$1/2$ lb	fresh bay scallops
1 pt	cherry tomatoes
$1/4$ C	dry white wine
$1/4$ C	vegetable oil
3 Tbsp	lemon juice
dash	garlic powder
to taste	black pepper
4	skewers

1. Parboil green peppers for 2 minutes.

2. Alternately thread first three ingredients on skewers.

3. Combine next five ingredients.

4. Brush kabobs with wine/oil/lemon mixture, then place on grill (or under broiler).

5. Grill for 15 minutes, turning and basting frequently.

Yield: 4 servings
Serving size: 1 kabob (6 oz)
Each serving provides:
Calories: 224
Total fat: 6 g
Saturated fat: 1 g
Cholesterol: 43 mg
Sodium: 355 mg
Total fiber: 3 g
Protein: 30 g
Carbohydrates: 13 g
Potassium: 993 mg

79

Spicy Baked Fish

This spicy seafood dish will delight everyone.

1 lb	cod (or other fish) fillet
1 Tbsp	olive oil
1 tsp	commercial spicy seasoning, salt free, or Hot 'N Spicy Seasoning mix (see recipe, page 140)
as needed	nonstick cooking spray

1. Preheat oven to 350 °F. Spray casserole dish with nonstick cooking oil spray.

2. Wash and dry fish. Place in dish. Drizzle with oil and seasoning mixture.

3. Bake uncovered for 15 minutes or until fish flakes with fork. Cut into 4 pieces. Serve with rice.

Yields: 4 servings
Serving size:
1 piece (3 oz)
Each serving provides:
Calories: 134
Total fat: 5 g
Saturated fat: 1 g
Cholesterol: 60 mg
Sodium: 93 mg
Total fiber: 0 g
Protein: 21 g
Carbohydrates: less than 1 g
Potassium: 309 mg

Spinach-Stuffed Sole

Heart healthy doesn't have to mean plain cooking, as this special dish shows.

1 tsp	olive oil
1/2 lb	fresh mushrooms, sliced
1/2 lb	fresh spinach, chopped
1/4 tsp	oregano leaves, crushed
1 clove	garlic, minced
1 1/2 lb	sole fillets or other white fish
2 Tbsp	sherry
4 oz	(1 C) part-skim mozzarella cheese, grated
as needed	nonstick cooking spray

1. Preheat oven to 400 °F.

2. Coat 10- by 6-inch baking dish with nonstick cooking spray.

3. Heat oil in skillet and sauté mushrooms for about 3 minutes or until tender.

4. Add spinach and continue cooking for about 1 minute or until spinach is barely wilted. Remove from heat and drain liquid into prepared baking dish.

5. Add oregano and garlic to drained sautéed vegetables. Stir to mix ingredients.

6. Divide vegetable mixture evenly among fillets and place in center of each.

7. Roll each fillet around mixture and place seam-side down in prepared baking dish.

8. Sprinkle with sherry, then grated mozzarella cheese. Bake for 15–20 minutes or until fish flakes easily. Lift out with slotted spoon.

Yield: 4 servings
Serving size: 1 fillet roll
Each serving provides:
Calories: 273
Total fat: 9 g
Saturated fat: 4 g
Cholesterol: 95 mg
Sodium: 163 mg
Total fiber: 2 g
Protein: 39 g
Carbohydrates: 6 g
Potassium: 880 mg

Tuna Salad

Perfect for a healthy lunchtime salad plate or sandwich.

2 can	(6 oz each) tuna, water pack
$1/2$ C	raw celery, chopped
$1/3$ C	green onions, chopped
$6^1/2$ Tbsp	mayonnaise, reduced fat

1. Rinse and drain tuna for 5 minutes. Break apart with fork.

2. Add celery, onion, and mayonnaise, and mix well.

Makes: 5 servings
Serving size: $1/2$ cup
Each serving provides:
Calories: 146
Total fat: 7 g
Saturated fat: 1 g
Cholesterol: 25 mg
Sodium: 158 mg
Total fiber: 1 g
Protein: 16 g
Carbohydrates: 4 g
Potassium: 201 mg

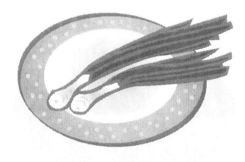

Chillin' Out Pasta Salad

Cook up this taste feast and set the table for a new family favorite.

2¹/₂ C	(8 oz) medium shell pasta
1 C	(8 oz) plain nonfat yogurt
2 Tbsp	spicy brown mustard
2 Tbsp	salt free herb seasoning
1¹/₂ C	celery, chopped
1 C	green onion, sliced
1 lb	small shrimp, cooked
3 C	(about 3 large) tomatoes, coarsely chopped

1. Cook pasta according to directions—but do not add salt to water. Drain and cool.

2. In large bowl, stir together yogurt, mustard, and herb seasoning.

3. Add pasta, celery, and green onion, and mix well. Chill for at least 2 hours.

4. Just before serving, carefully stir in shrimp and tomatoes.

Servings: 12
Serving size: ¹/₂ cup
Each serving yields:
Calories: 140
Total fat: 1 g
Saturated fat: less than 1 g
Cholesterol: 60 mg
Sodium: 135 mg
Total fiber: 1 g
Protein: 14 g
Carbohydrates: 19 g
Potassium: 295 mg

Classic Macaroni and Cheese

This recipe proves you don't have to give up your favorite dishes to eat heart healthy meals. Here's a lower fat version of a true classic.

2 C	macaroni
1/2 C	onions, chopped
1/2 C	evaporated skim milk
1	medium egg, beaten
1/4 tsp	black pepper
1 1/4 C	(4 oz) lowfat sharp cheddar cheese, finely shredded
as needed	nonstick cooking spray

1. Cook macaroni according to directions—but do not add salt to the cooking water. Drain and set aside.

2. Spray casserole dish with nonstick cooking spray.

3. Preheat oven to 350 °F.

4. Lightly spray saucepan with nonstick cooking spray.
   Add onions to saucepan and sauté for about 3 minutes.

5. In another bowl, combine macaroni, onions, and rest of the ingredients, and mix thoroughly.

6. Transfer mixture into casserole dish.

7. Bake for 25 minutes or until bubbly.
   Let stand for 10 minutes before serving.

Servings: 8
Serving size: 1/2 cup
Each serving provides:
Calories: 200
Total fat: 4 g
Saturated fat: 2 g
Cholesterol: 34 mg
Sodium: 120 mg
Total fiber: 1 g
Protein: 11 g
Carbohydrates: 29 g
Potassium: 119 mg

Red Hot Fusilli

This lively dish is low in saturated fat and free of cholesterol.

1 Tbsp	olive oil
2 cloves	garlic, minced
$1/4$ C	fresh parsley, minced
4 C	ripe tomatoes, chopped
1 Tbsp	fresh basil, chopped (or 1 tsp dried)
1 Tbsp	oregano leaves, crushed (or 1 tsp dried)
$1/4$ tsp	salt
to taste	ground red pepper or cayenne
8 oz	uncooked fusilli pasta (4 C cooked)
$1/2$ lb	(optional) cooked chicken breasts, diced into $1/2$-inch pieces ($3/4$ lb if raw)

Yield: 4 servings
Serving Size: 1 cup
Each serving provides:
Calories: 293
Total fat: 5 g
Saturated fat: 1 g
Cholesterol: 0 mg
Sodium: 168 mg
Total fiber: 4 g
Protein: 9 g
Carbohydrates: 54 g
Potassium: 489 mg

1. Heat oil in medium saucepan. Sauté garlic and parsley until golden.

2. Add tomatoes and spices. Cook uncovered over low heat for 15 minutes or until thickened, stirring frequently. If desired, add chicken and continue cooking for 15 minutes until chicken is heated through and sauce is thick.

3. Cook pasta in unsalted water until firm.

4. To serve, spoon sauce over pasta and sprinkle with coarsely chopped parsley. Serve hot as a main dish and cold for next day's lunch.

Each serving with chicken provides:
Calories: 391
Total fat: 8 g
Saturated fat: 1 g
Cholesterol: 48 mg
Sodium: 211 mg
Total fiber: 4 g
Protein: 27 g
Carbohydrates: 54 g
Postassium: 629 mg

Sweet and Sour Seashells

Drain the marinade before serving this dish in order to lower the fat and sodium—but keep all the great taste.

1 lb	uncooked small seashell pasta (9 C cooked)
2 Tbsp	vegetable oil
3/4 C	sugar
1/2 C	cider vinegar
1/2 C	wine vinegar
1/2 C	water
3 Tbsp	prepared mustard
to taste	black pepper
1 jar	(2 oz) sliced pimentos
2	small cucumbers
2	small onions, thinly sliced
18 leaves	lettuce

1. Cook pasta in unsalted water, drain, rinse with cold water, and drain again. Stir in oil.

2. Transfer to 4-quart bowl. In blender, place sugar, vinegars, water, prepared mustard, salt, pepper, and pimento. Process at low speed for 15–20 seconds, or just enough so flecks of pimento can be seen. Pour over pasta.

3. Score cucumber peel with fork tines. Cut cucumber in half lengthwise, then slice thinly. Add to pasta with onion slices. Toss well.

4. Marinate, covered, in refrigerator for 24 hours. Stir occasionally.

5. Drain, and serve on lettuce.

Yield: 18 servings
Serving Size: 1/2 cup
Each serving provides:
Calories: 158
Total fat: 2 g
Saturated fat: less than 1 g
Cholesterol: 0 mg
Sodium: 35 mg
Total fiber: 2 g
Protein: 4 g
Carbohydrates: 31 g
Potassium: 150 mg

Black Beans With Rice

A delicious Caribbean favorite that's made with very little added fat.

1 lb	black beans, dry
7 C	water
1	medium green pepper, coarsely chopped
1 1/2 C	onion, chopped
1 Tbsp	vegetable oil
2	bay leaves
1 clove	garlic, minced
1/2 tsp	salt
1 Tbsp	vinegar (or lemon juice)
6 C	rice, cooked in unsalted water
1 jar	(4 oz) sliced pimento, drained
1	lemon, cut into wedges

1. Pick through beans to remove bad ones. Soak beans overnight in cold water. Drain and rinse.

2. In large soup pot or Dutch oven, stir together beans, water, green pepper, onion, oil, bay leaves, garlic, and salt. Cover and boil for 1 hour.

3. Reduce heat and simmer, covered, for 3–4 hours or until beans are very tender. Stir occasionally, and add water if needed.

4. Remove and mash about a third of beans. Return to pot. Stir and heat through.

5. When ready to serve, remove bay leaves and stir in vinegar or lemon juice.

6. Serve over rice. Garnish with sliced pimento and lemon wedges.

Yield: 6 servings
Serving size: 8 oz
Each serving provides:
Calories: 508
Total fat: 4 g
Saturated fat: 1 g
Cholesterol: 0 mg
Sodium: 206 mg
Total fiber: 14 g
Protein: 21 g
Carbohydrates: 98 g
Potassium: 852 mg

Caribbean Pink Beans

This dish stays healthy by using beans prepared without lard or other fat.

1 lb	pink beans
10 C	water
2	medium plantains, finely chopped
1	large tomato, finely chopped
1	small red pepper, finely chopped
1	medium white onion, finely chopped
3 cloves	garlic, finely chopped
1^1/$_2$ tsp	salt

▶SERVING TIP

Try it with rice.

1. Rinse and pick through beans. Put beans in large pot and add 10 cups of water. Place pot in refrigerator and allow beans to soak overnight.

2. Cook beans until soft. Add more water, as needed, while beans are cooking.

3. Add plantains, tomato, pepper, onion, garlic, and salt. Continue cooking at low heat until plantains are soft.

Yield: 16 servings
Serving size: ^{1}/$_2$ cup
Each serving provides:
Calories: 133
Total fat: less than 1 g
Saturated fat: less than 1 g
Cholesterol: 0 mg
Sodium: 205 mg
Total fiber: 5 g
Protein: 6 g
Carbohydrates: 28 g
Potassium: 495 mg

New Orleans Red Beans

This vegetarian dish is virtually fat free and entirely delicious.

1 lb	dry red beans
2 qt	water
1 1/2 C	onion, chopped
1 C	celery, chopped
4	bay leaves
1 C	green peppers, chopped
3 Tbsp	garlic, chopped
3 Tbsp	parsley, chopped
2 tsp	dried thyme, crushed
1 tsp	salt
1 tsp	black pepper

1. Pick through beans to remove bad ones. Rinse beans rinse thoroughly.

2. In large pot, combine beans, water, onion, celery, and bay leaves. Bring to boil. Reduce heat, cover, and cook over low heat for about 1 1/2 hours or until beans are tender. Stir. Mash beans against side of pan.

3. Add green pepper, garlic, parsley, thyme, salt, and black pepper. Cook uncovered over low heat until creamy, about 30 minutes. Remove bay leaves.

4. Serve with hot cooked brown rice, if desired.

Yield: 8 servings
Serving size: 1 1/4 cup
Each serving provides:
Calories: 171
Total fat: less than 1 g
Saturated fat: less than 1 g
Cholesterol: 0 mg
Sodium: 285 mg
Total fiber: 7 g
Protein: 10 g
Carbohydrates: 32 g
Potassium: 665 mg

Summer Vegetable Spaghetti

This lively vegetarian pasta dish is delicious hot or cold.

2 C	small yellow onions, cut in eighths
2 C	(about 1 lb) ripe tomatoes, peeled, chopped
2 C	(about 1 lb) yellow and green squash, thinly sliced
1^1/2 C	(about ^{1}/2 lb) fresh green beans, cut
^{2}/3 C	water
2 Tbsp	fresh parsley, minced
1 clove	garlic, minced
^{1}/2 tsp	chili powder
^{1}/4 tsp	salt
to taste	black pepper
1 can	(6 oz) tomato paste
1 lb	spaghetti, uncooked
^{1}/2 C	Parmesan cheese, grated

1. Combine first 10 ingredients in large saucepan. Cook for 10 minutes, then stir in tomato paste. Cover and cook gently for 15 minutes, stirring occasionally, until vegetables are tender.

2. Cook spaghetti in unsalted water according to package directions.

3. Spoon sauce over drained hot spaghetti. Sprinkle Parmesan cheese on top.

Yield: 9 servings
Serving size: 1 cup of spaghetti and ^{3}/4 cup of sauce with vegetables
Each serving provides:
Calories: 271
Total fat: 3 g
Saturated fat: 1 g
Cholesterol: 4 mg
Sodium: 328 mg
Total fiber: 5 g
Protein: 11 g
Carbohydrates: 51 g
Potassium: 436 mg

Vegetarian Spaghetti Sauce

Simple and simply delicious—here's a healthy sauce to serve with spaghetti or other pasta.

2 Tbsp	olive oil
2	small onions, chopped
3 cloves	garlic, chopped
1¹/₄ C	zucchini, sliced
1 Tbsp	oregano, dried
1 Tbsp	basil, dried
1 can	(8 oz) tomato sauce
1 can	(6 oz) tomato paste*
2	medium tomatoes, chopped
1 C	water

*Reduce sodium by using 6-oz can of no salt added tomato paste. New sodium content for each serving is 260 mg.

1. In medium skillet, heat oil. Sauté onions, garlic, and zucchini in oil for 5 minutes on medium heat.

2. Add remaining ingredients and simmer, covered, for 45 minutes. Serve over spaghetti.

Yield: 6 servings
Serving size: ³/₄ cup
Each serving provides:
Calories: 102
Total fat: 5 g
Saturated fat: 1 g
Cholesterol: 0 mg
Sodium: 459 mg
Total fiber: 5 g
Protein: 3 g
Carbohydrates: 14 g
Potassium: 623 mg

Zucchini Lasagna

Say, "Cheese," because this healthy version of a favorite comfort food will leave you smiling.

$1/2$ lb	lasagna noodles, cooked in unsalted water
$3/4$ C	part-skim mozzarella cheese, grated
$1^1/2$ C	fat free cottage cheese*
$1/4$ C	Parmesan cheese, grated
$1^1/2$ C	raw zucchini, sliced
$2^1/2$ C	no salt added tomato sauce
2 tsp	basil, dried
2 tsp	oregano, dried
$1/4$ C	onion, chopped
1 clove	garlic
$1/8$ tsp	black pepper

*Use unsalted cottage cheese to reduce the sodium content. New sodium content for each serving is 196 mg.

Yield: 6 servings
Serving size: 1 piece
Each serving provides:
Calories: 276
Total fat: 5 g
Saturated fat: 2 g
Cholesterol: 11 mg
Sodium: 380 mg
Total fiber: 5 g
Protein: 19 g
Carbohydrates: 41 g
Potassium: 561 mg

1. Preheat oven to 350 °F. Lightly spray 9- by 13-inch baking dish with vegetable oil spray.

2. In small bowl, combine $1/8$ cup mozzarella and 1 tablespoon Parmesan cheese. Set aside.

3. In medium bowl, combine remaining mozzarella and Parmesan cheese with all of the cottage cheese. Mix well and set aside.

4. Combine tomato sauce with remaining ingredients. Spread thin layer of tomato sauce in bottom of baking dish. Add a third of noodles in single layer. Spread half of cottage cheese mixture on top. Add layer of zucchini.

5. Repeat layering. Add thin coating of sauce. Top with noodles, sauce, and reserved cheese mixture. Cover with aluminum foil.

6. Bake for 30–40 minutes. Cool for 10–15 minutes. Cut into 6 portions.

SIDE DISHES

Fresh Cabbage and Tomato Salad

Tempt your children to eat more vegetables with this refreshing, tasty salad.

1 head	small cabbage, sliced thinly
2	medium tomatoes, cut in cubes
1 C	radishes, sliced
1/4 tsp	salt
2 tsp	olive oil
2 Tbsp	rice vinegar (or lemon juice)
1/2 tsp	black pepper
1/2 tsp	red pepper
2 Tbsp	fresh cilantro, chopped

1. In large bowl, mix together cabbage, tomatoes, and radishes.

2. In another bowl, mix together the rest of the ingredients and pour over vegetables.

Yield: 8 servings
Serving size: 1 cup
Each serving provides:
Calories: 43
Total fat: 1 g
Saturated fat: less than 1 g
Cholesterol: 0 mg
Sodium: 88 mg
Total fiber: 3 g
Protein: 2 g
Carbohydrates: 7 g
Potassium: 331 mg

Green Beans Sauté

In this dish, green beans and onions are lightly sautéed in just 1 tablespoon of oil.

1 lb	fresh or frozen green beans, cut in 1-inch pieces
1 Tbsp	vegetable oil
1	large yellow onion, halved lengthwise, thinly sliced
$1/2$ tsp	salt
$1/8$ tsp	black pepper
1 Tbsp	fresh parsley, minced

1. If using fresh green beans, cook in boiling water for 10–12 minutes or steam for 2–3 minutes until barely fork tender. Drain well. If using frozen green beans, thaw first.

2. Heat oil in large skillet. Sauté onion until golden.

3. Stir in green beans, salt, and pepper. Heat through.

4. Before serving, toss with parsley.

Yield: 4 servings
Serving Size: $1/4$ cup
Each serving provides:
Calories: 64
Total fat: 4 g
Saturated fat: less than 1 g
Cholesterol: 0 mg
Sodium: 282 mg
Total fiber: 3 g
Protein: 2 g
Carbohydrates: 8 g
Potassium: 161 mg

Italian Vegetable Bake

Try this colorful, low-sodium baked dish, prepared without added fat.

1 can	(28 oz) tomatoes, whole
1	medium onion, sliced
$1/2$ lb	fresh green beans, sliced
$1/2$ lb	fresh okra, cut into $1/2$-inch pieces (or $1/2$ of 10-oz package frozen, cut)
$3/4$ C	green pepper, finely chopped
2 Tbsp	lemon juice
1 Tbsp	fresh basil, chopped, or 1 tsp dried basil, crushed
$1 1/2$ tsp	fresh oregano leaves, chopped (or $1/2$ tsp dried oregano, crushed)
3	medium (7-inch-long) zucchini, cut into 1-inch cubes
1	medium eggplant, pared, cut into 1-inch cubes
2 Tbsp	Parmesan cheese, grated

1. Drain and coarsely chop tomatoes. Save liquid. Mix together tomatoes, reserved liquid, onion, green beans, okra, green pepper, lemon juice, and herbs. Cover and bake at 325 °F for 15 minutes.

2. Mix in zucchini and eggplant. Continue baking, covered, 60–70 minutes more or until vegetables are tender. Stir occasionally.

3. Just before serving, sprinkle top with Parmesan cheese.

Yield: 18 servings
Serving Size: $1/2$ cup
Each serving provides:
Calories: 27
Total fat: less than 1 g
Saturated fat: less than 1 g
Cholesterol: 1 mg
Sodium: 86 mg
Total fiber: 2 g
Protein: 2 g
Carbohydrates: 5 g
Potassium: 244 mg

Limas and Spinach

Your family will love vegetables cooked this way.

2 C	frozen lima beans
1 Tbsp	vegetable oil
1 C	fennel, cut in 4-oz strips
$1/2$ C	onion, chopped
$1/4$ C	low-sodium chicken broth
4 C	leaf spinach, washed thoroughly
1 Tbsp	distilled vinegar
$1/8$ tsp	black pepper
1 Tbsp	raw chives

1. Steam or boil lima beans in unsalted water for about 10 minutes. Drain.

2. In skillet, sauté onions and fennel in oil.

3. Add beans and stock to onions and cover. Cook for 2 minutes.

4. Stir in spinach. Cover and cook until spinach has wilted, about 2 minutes.

5. Stir in vinegar and pepper. Cover and let stand for 30 seconds.

6. Sprinkle with chives and serve.

Yield: Makes 7 servings
Serving size: $1/2$ cup
Each serving provides:
Calories: 93
Total fat: 2 g
Saturated fat: less than 1 g
Cholesterol: 0 mg
Sodium: 84 mg
Total fiber: 6 g
Protein: 5 g
Carbohydrates: 15 g
Potassium: 452 mg

Smothered Greens

These healthy greens get their rich flavor from smoked turkey, instead of fatback.

3 C	water
1/4 lb	smoked turkey breast, skinless
1 Tbsp	fresh hot pepper, chopped
1/4 tsp	cayenne pepper
1/4 tsp	cloves, ground
2 cloves	garlic, crushed
1/2 tsp	thyme
1 stalk	scallion, chopped
1 tsp	ginger, ground
1/4 C	onion, chopped
2 lb	greens (mustard, turnip, collard, kale, or mixture)

1. Place all ingredients except greens into large saucepan and bring to boil.

2. Prepare greens by washing thoroughly and removing stems.

3. Tear or slice leaves into bite-size pieces.

4. Add greens to turkey stock. Cook for 20–30 minutes until tender.

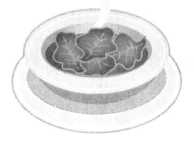

Yield: 5 servings
Serving size: 1 cup
Each serving provides:
Calories: 80
Total fat: 2 g
Saturated fat: less than 1 g
Cholesterol: 16 mg
Sodium: 378 mg
Total fiber: 4 g
Protein: 9 g
Carbohydrates: 9 g
Potassium: 472 mg

Vegetable Stew

Here's a great new way to use summer vegetables.

3 C	water
1 cube	vegetable bouillon, low sodium
2 C	white potatoes, cut in 2-inch strips
2 C	carrots, sliced
4 C	summer squash, cut in 1-inch squares
1 C	summer squash, cut in 4 chunks
1 can	(15 oz) sweet corn, rinsed, drained (or 2 ears fresh corn, 1 $1/2$ C)
1 tsp	thyme
2 cloves	garlic, minced
1 stalk	scallion, chopped
$1/2$	small hot pepper, chopped
1 C	onion, coarsely chopped
1 C	tomatoes, diced (add other favorite vegetables, such as broccoli and cauliflower)

Yield: Makes 8 servings
Serving size: 1$1/4$ cups
Each serving provides:
Calories: 119
Total fat: 1 g
Saturated fat: less than 1 g
Cholesterol: 0 mg
Sodium: 196 mg
Total fiber: 4 g
Protein: 4 g
Carbohydrates: 27 g
Potassium: 524 mg

1. Put water and bouillon in large pot and bring to a boil.

2. Add potatoes and carrots, and simmer for 5 minutes.

3. Add remaining ingredients, except for tomatoes, and continue cooking for 15 minutes over medium heat.

4. Remove four chunks of squash and puree in blender.

5. Return pureed mixture to pot and let cook for 10 minutes more.

6. Add tomatoes and cook for another 5 minutes.

7. Remove from flame and let sit for 10 minutes to allow stew to thicken.

Vegetables With a Touch of Lemon

This heart healthy sauce uses lemon juice and herbs for a tangy taste.

1/2 head	small cauliflower, cut into florets
2 C	broccoli, cut into florets
2 Tbsp	lemon juice
1 Tbsp	olive oil
1 clove	garlic, minced
2 tsp	fresh parsley, chopped

1. Steam broccoli and cauliflower until tender (about 10 minutes).

2. In small saucepan, mix the lemon juice, oil, and garlic, and cook over low heat for 2 or 3 minutes.

3. Put vegetables in serving dish. Pour lemon sauce over them. Garnish with parsley.

Yield: 6 servings
Serving size: 1/2 cup
Each serving provides:
Calories: 22
Total fat: 2 g
Saturated fat: less than 1 g
Cholesterol: 0 mg
Sodium: 7 mg
Total fiber: 1 g
Protein: 1 g
Carbohydrates: 2 g
Potassium: 49 mg

Candied Yams

A bit of margarine and some orange juice make this dish sweet.

3	(1 $1/2$ C) medium yams
$1/4$ C	brown sugar, packed
1 tsp	flour, sifted
$1/4$ tsp	salt
$1/4$ tsp	ground cinnamon
$1/4$ tsp	ground nutmeg
$1/4$ tsp	orange peel
1 tsp	soft tub margarine
$1/2$ C	orange juice

1. Cut yams in half and boil until tender but firm (about 20 minutes). When cool enough to handle, peel and slice into $1/4$-inch thickness.

2. Combine sugar, flour, salt, cinnamon, nutmeg, and grated orange peel.

3. Place half of sliced yams in medium-size casserole dish. Sprinkle with spiced sugar mixture.

4. Dot with half the amount of margarine.

5. Add second layer of yams, using the rest of the ingredients in the same order as above. Add orange juice.

6. Bake uncovered for 20 minutes in oven that was preheated to 350 °F.

Yield: 6 servings
Serving size: $1/4$ cup
Each serving provides:
Calories: 110
Total fat: less than 1 g
Saturated fat: less than 1 g
Cholesterol: 0 mg
Sodium: 115 mg
Total fiber: 2 g
Protein: 1 g
Carbohydrates: 25 g
Potassium: 344 mg

Delicious Oven French Fries

Find french fries hard to resist? Here's a version to give in to.

4	(2 lb) large potatoes
8 C	ice water
1 tsp	garlic powder
1 tsp	onion powder
$1/4$ tsp	salt
1 tsp	white pepper
$1/4$ tsp	allspice
1 tsp	hot pepper flakes
1 Tbsp	vegetable oil

1. Scrub potatoes and cut into $1/2$-inch strips.

2. Place potato strips into ice water, cover, and chill for 1 hour or longer.

3. Remove potatoes and dry strips thoroughly.

4. Place garlic powder, onion powder, salt, white pepper, allspice, and pepper flakes in plastic bag.

5. Toss potatoes in spice mixture.

6. Brush potatoes with oil.

7. Place potatoes in nonstick shallow baking pan.

8. Cover with aluminum foil and place in 475 °F oven for 15 minutes.

9. Remove foil and continue baking uncovered for additional 15–20 minutes or until golden brown. Turn fries occasionally to brown on all sides.

Yield: 5 servings
Serving size: 1 cup
Each serving provides:
Calories: 238
Total fat: 4 g
Saturated fat: 1 g
Cholesterol: 0 mg
Sodium: 163 mg
Total fiber: 5 g
Protein: 5 g
Carbohydrates: 48 g
Potassium: 796 mg

Garden Potato Salad

Lowfat cottage cheese is the secret ingredient in this delicious dish.

6	(about 3 lb) large potatoes, boiled in jackets, peeled, cut into 4-inch cubes
1 C	celery, chopped
1/2 C	green onion, sliced
2 Tbsp	parsley, chopped
1 C	lowfat cottage cheese
3/4 C	skim milk
3 Tbsp	lemon juice
2 Tbsp	cider vinegar
1/2 tsp	celery seed
1/2 tsp	dill weed
1/2 tsp	dry mustard
1/2 tsp	white pepper

1. In large bowl, place potatoes, celery, green onion, and parsley.

2. Meanwhile, in blender or food processor, blend cottage cheese, milk, lemon juice, vinegar, celery seed, dill weed, dry mustard, and white pepper until smooth. Chill for 1 hour.

3. Pour chilled cottage cheese mixture over vegetables and mix well. Chill at least 30 minutes before serving.

Yield: 10 servings
Serving size: 1 cup
Each serving provides:
Calories: 145
Total fat: 1 g
Saturated fat: less than 1 g
Cholesterol: 2 mg
Sodium: 122 mg
Total fiber: 3 g
Protein: 6 g
Carbohydrates: 29 g
Potassium: 543 mg

Garlic Mashed Potatoes

2	(1 lb) large potatoes, peeled, quartered
2 C	skim milk
2 cloves	garlic, large, chopped
1/2 tsp	white pepper

Whether with saucepan or microwave, you can make this dish tasty without added fat or salt.

To use saucepan:

1. Cook potatoes, covered, in small amount of boiling water for 20–25 minutes or until tender. Remove from heat. Drain and recover.

2. Meanwhile, in small saucepan over low heat, cook garlic in milk until soft (about 30 minutes).

3. Add milk-garlic mixture and white pepper to potatoes. Beat with electric mixer on low speed, or mash with potato masher, until smooth.

To use microwave:

1. Scrub potatoes, pat dry, and prick with fork.

2. On plate, cook potatoes uncovered on 100 percent (high) power until tender (about 12 minutes), turning over once.

3. Let stand 5 minutes, then peel and quarter.

4. Meanwhile, in 4-cup measuring glass, combine milk and garlic. Cook, uncovered, on 50 percent (medium) power until garlic is soft (about 4 minutes).

5. Continue as directed above.

Yield: 4 servings
Serving size: 3/4 cup
Each serving provides:
Calories: 142
Total fat: less than 1 g
Saturated fat: less than 1 g
Cholesterol: 2 mg
Sodium: 69 mg
Total fiber: 2 g
Protein: 6 g
Carbohydrates: 29 g
Potassium: 577 mg

New Potato Salad

Onions and spices give this very low-sodium dish plenty of zip.

16	(5 C) small new potatoes
2 Tbsp	olive oil
$1/4$ C	green onions, chopped
$1/4$ tsp	black pepper
1 tsp	dill weed, dried

1. Thoroughly clean potatoes with vegetable brush and water.
2. Boil potatoes for 20 minutes or until tender.
3. Drain and cool potatoes for 20 minutes.
4. Cut potatoes into fourths and mix with olive oil, onions, and spices.
5. Refrigerate and serve.

Yield: 5 servings
Serving size: 1 cup
Each serving provides:
Calories: 187
Total fat: 6 g
Saturated fat: 1 g
Cholesterol: 0 mg
Sodium: 12 mg
Total fiber: 3 g
Protein: 3 g
Carbohydrates: 32 g
Potassium: 547 mg

Savory Potato Salad

Here's a potato salad that's both traditional and new—with a high taste-lowfat twist.

6	(about 2 lb) medium potatoes
2 stalks	celery, finely chopped
2 stalks	scallion, finely chopped
1/4 C	red bell pepper, coarsely chopped
1/4 C	green bell pepper, coarsely chopped
1 Tbsp	onion, finely chopped
1	egg, hard boiled, chopped
6 Tbsp	light mayonnaise
1 tsp	mustard
1/2 tsp	salt
1/4 tsp	black pepper
1/4 tsp	dill weed, dried

1. Wash potatoes, cut in half, and place in saucepan in cold water.

2. Cook covered over medium heat for 25–30 minutes or until tender.

3. Drain and dice potatoes when cool.

4. Add vegetables and egg to potatoes, and toss.

5. Blend together mayonnaise, mustard, salt, pepper, and dill weed.

6. Pour dressing over potato mixture, and stir gently to coat evenly.

7. Chill for at least 1 hour before serving.

Yield: 10 servings.
Serving size: 1/2 cup
Each serving provides:
Calories: 98
Total fat: 2 g
Saturated fat: less than 1 g
Cholesterol: 21 mg
Sodium: 212 mg
Total fiber: 2 g
Protein: 2 g
Carbohydrates: 18 g
Potassium: 291 mg

106

Sweet Potato Custard

Sweet potatoes and bananas make this lowfat custard a dessert-lover's delight.

1 C	sweet potato, cooked, mashed
$1/2$ C	(about 2) small bananas, mashed
1 C	evaporated skim milk
2 Tbsp	brown sugar, packed
2	egg yolks (or $1/3$ C egg substitute), beaten
$1/2$ tsp	salt
$1/4$ C	raisins
1 Tbsp	sugar
1 tsp	ground cinnamon
as needed	nonstick cooking spray

1. In medium bowl, stir together sweet potato and banana.

2. Add milk, blending well.

3. Add brown sugar, egg yolks, and salt, mixing thoroughly.

4. Spray 1-quart casserole with nonstick cooking spray. Transfer sweet potato mixture to casserole dish.

5. Combine raisins, sugar, and cinnamon. Sprinkle over top of sweet potato mixture.

6. Bake in preheated 325 °F oven for 40–45 minutes or until knife inserted near center comes out clean.

Yield: 6 servings
Serving size: $1/2$ cup
Each serving provides:
Calories: 160
Total fat: 2 g
Saturated fat: 1 g
Cholesterol: 72 mg*
Sodium: 255 mg
Total fiber : 2 g
Protein: 5 g
Carbohydrates: 32 g
Potassium: 488 mg

*If using egg substitute, cholesterol will be lower.

Wonderful Stuffed Potatoes

Here's a lavish-tasting lowfat, low-cholesterol, low-sodium treat.

4	medium baking potatoes
3/4 C	lowfat (1%) cottage cheese
1/4 C	lowfat (1%) milk
2 Tbsp	soft margarine
1 tsp	dill weed
3/4 tsp	herb seasoning
4-6 drops	hot pepper sauce
2 tsp	Parmesan cheese, grated

1. Prick potatoes with fork. Bake at 425 °F for 60 minutes or until fork is easily inserted.

2. Cut potatoes in half lengthwise. Carefully scoop out potato, leaving about 1/2 inch of pulp inside shell. Mash pulp in large bowl.

3. By hand, mix in remaining ingredients, except Parmesan cheese. Spoon mixture into potato shells.

4. Sprinkle each top with 1/4 teaspoon Parmesan cheese.

5. Place on baking sheet and return to oven. Bake for 15–20 minutes or until tops are golden brown.

Yield: 8 servings
Serving size: 1/2 potato
Each serving provides:
Calories: 113
Total fat: 3 g
Saturated fat: 1 g
Cholesterol: 1 mg
Sodium: 151 mg
Total fiber: 2 g
Protein: 5 g
Carbohydrates: 17 g
Potassium: 293 mg

Oriental Rice

1¹/2 C	water
1 C	chicken stock or broth, fat skimmed from top
1¹/3 C	long grain white rice, uncooked
2 tsp	vegetable oil
2 Tbsp	onion, finely chopped
1 C	celery, finely chopped
2 Tbsp	green pepper, finely chopped
¹/2 C	pecans, chopped
¹/4 tsp	ground sage
¹/2 C	water chestnuts, sliced
¹/4 tsp	nutmeg
to taste	black pepper

Skim off the fat from the chicken stock, use a minimum of oil, and don't add salt—and you'll create a dish that's flavorful and healthy.

1. Bring water and stock to boil in medium-size saucepan.

2. Add rice and stir. Cover and simmer for 20 minutes.

3. Remove pan from heat. Let stand, covered, for 5 minutes or until all liquid is absorbed. Reserve.

4. Heat oil in large nonstick skillet.

5. Sauté onion and celery over moderate heat for 3 minutes. Stir in remaining ingredients, including reserved cooked rice. Fluff with fork before serving.

Yield: 10 servings
Serving size: ¹/2 cup
Each serving provides:
Calories: 139
Total fat: 5 g
Saturated fat: less than 1 g
Cholesterol: 0 mg
Sodium: 86 mg
Total fiber: 1 g
Protein: 3 g
Carbohydrates: 21 g
Potassium: 124 mg

Parmesan Rice and Pasta Pilaf

Is it pilaf? Is it pasta? This dish is both—and healthy and tasty too.

2 Tbsp	olive oil
1/2 C	vermicelli, finely broken, uncooked
2 Tbsp	onion, diced
1 C	long grain white rice, uncooked
1 1/4 C	chicken stock, hot
1 1/4 C	water, hot
1/4 tsp	ground white pepper
1	bay leaf
2 Tbsp	Parmesan cheese, grated

1. In large skillet, heat oil. Sauté vermicelli and onion until golden brown (about 2–4 minutes) over medium-high heat. Drain off oil.

2. Add rice, stock, water, pepper, and bay leaf. Cover and simmer for 15–20 minutes. Fluff with fork. Cover and let stand for 5–20 minutes. Remove bay leaf.

3. Sprinkle with cheese, and serve immediately.

Yield: 6 servings
Serving size: 2/3 cup
Each serving provides:
Calories: 208
Total fat: 6 g
Saturated fat: 1 g
Cholesterol: 2 mg
Sodium: 140 mg
Total fiber: 1 g
Protein: 5 g
Carbohydrates: 33 g
Potassium: 90 mg

Sunshine Rice

1¹/2 Tbsp	vegetable oil
1¹/4 C	celery, finely chopped, with leaves
1¹/2 C	onion, finely chopped
1 C	water
¹/2 C	orange juice
2 Tbsp	lemon juice
dash	hot sauce
1 C	long grain white rice, uncooked
¹/4 C	slivered almonds

A citrus taste, combined with almonds, celery, and onions—but no added salt—make this side dish a new classic. Try it with fish.

1. Heat oil in medium saucepan. Add celery and onions, and sauté until tender (about 10 minutes).

2. Add water, juices, and hot sauce. Bring to boil. Stir in rice and bring back to boil. Let stand covered until rice is tender and liquid is absorbed.

3. Stir in almonds. Serve immediately.

Yield: 4 servings
Serving size: ¹/3 cup
Each serving provides:
Calories: 276
Total fat: 6 g
Saturated fat: 1 g
Cholesterol: 0 mg
Sodium: 52 mg
Total fiber: 5 g
Protein: 7 g
Carbohydrates: 50 g
Potassium: 406 mg

BREADS

Apricot-Orange Bread

This bread is low in all the right places— saturated fat, cholesterol, and sodium—without losing any taste and texture.

1 package	(6 oz) dried apricots, cut into small pieces
2 C	water
2 Tbsp	margarine
1 C	sugar
1	egg, slightly beaten
1 Tbsp	orange peel, freshly grated
$3^1/_2$ C	all-purpose flour, sifted
$^1/_2$ C	fat free dry milk powder
2 tsp	baking powder
1 tsp	baking soda
1 tsp	salt
$^1/_2$ C	orange juice
$^1/_2$ C	pecans, chopped

Yield: 2 loaves
Serving size: $^1/_2$-inch slice
Each serving provides:
Calories: 97
Total fat: 2 g
Saturated fat: less than 1 g
Cholesterol: 6 mg
Sodium: 113 mg
Total fiber: 1 g
Protein: 2 g
Carbohydrates: 18 g
Potassium: 110 mg

1. Preheat oven to 350 °F. Lightly oil two, 9- by 5-inch loaf pans.

2. Cook apricots in water in covered medium-size saucepan for 10–15 minutes or until tender but not mushy. Drain and reserve 3/4 cup liquid. Set apricots aside to cool.

3. Cream together margarine and sugar. By hand, beat in egg and orange peel.

4. Sift together flour, dry milk, baking powder, soda, and salt. Add to creamed mixture alternately with reserved apricot liquid and orange juice.

5. Stir apricot pieces and pecans into batter.

6. Turn batter into prepared pans.

7. Bake for 40–45 minutes or until bread springs back when lightly touched in center.

8. Cool for 5 minutes in pans. Remove from pans and completely cool on wire rack before slicing.

Banana-Nut Bread

Bananas and lowfat buttermilk lower the fat for this old favorite, while keeping all the moistness.

1 C	ripe bananas, mashed
1/3 C	lowfat buttermilk
1/2 C	brown sugar, packed
1/4 C	margarine
1	egg
2 C	all-purpose flour, sifted
1 tsp	baking powder
1/2 tsp	baking soda
1/2 tsp	salt
1/2 C	pecans, chopped

1. Preheat oven to 350 °F. Lightly oil two, 9- by 5-inch loaf pans.

2. Stir together mashed bananas and buttermilk. Set aside.

3. Cream brown sugar and margarine together until light. Beat in egg. Add banana mixture and beat well.

4. Sift together flour, baking powder, baking soda, and salt. Add all at once to liquid ingredients. Stir until well blended.

5. Stir in nuts, and turn into prepared pans.

6. Bake for 50–55 minutes or until toothpick inserted in center comes out clean. Cool for 5 minutes in pans.

7. Remove from pans and complete cooling on a wire rack before slicing.

Yield: 2 loaves
Serving size: 1/2-inch slice
Each serving provides:
Calories: 133
Total fat: 5 g
Saturated fat: 1 g
Cholesterol: 12 mg
Sodium: 138 mg
Total fiber: 1 g
Protein: 2 g
Carbohydrates: 20 g
Potassium: 114 mg

Carrot-Raisin Bread

You don't need lots of oil and eggs to make a rich-tasting bread—as this recipe shows.

1 1/2 C	all-purpose flour, sifted
1/2 C	sugar
1 tsp	baking powder
1/4 tsp	baking soda
1/2 tsp	salt
1 1/2 tsp	ground cinnamon
1/4 tsp	ground allspice
1	egg, beaten
1/2 C	water
2 Tbsp	vegetable oil
1/2 tsp	vanilla
1 1/2 C	carrots, finely shredded
1/4 C	pecans, chopped
1/4 C	golden raisins

1. Preheat oven to 350 °F. Lightly oil two, 9- by 5-inch loaf pans.

2. Stir together dry ingredients in large mixing bowl. Make well in center of dry mixture.

3. In separate bowl, mix together remaining ingredients. Add mixture all at once to dry ingredients. Stir just enough to moisten and evenly distribute carrots.

4. Turn into prepared pan. Bake for 50 minutes or until toothpick inserted in center comes out clean.

5. Cool for 5 minutes in pan. Remove from pan and complete cooling on wire rack before slicing.

Yield: 2 loaves
Serving size: 1/2-inch slice
Each serving provides:
Calories: 99
Total fat: 3 g
Saturated fat: less than 1 g
Cholesterol: 12 mg
Sodium: 97 mg
Total fiber: 1 g
Protein: 2 g
Carbohydrates: 17 g
Potassium: 69 mg

Good-for-You Cornbread

This is not only good for you but also good in you—making it a healthy comfort food.

1 C	cornmeal
1 C	flour
$1/4$ C	white sugar
1 tsp	baking powder
1 C	1% fat buttermilk
1	egg, whole
$1/4$ C	tub margarine
1 tsp	vegetable oil (to grease baking pan)

1. Preheat oven to 350 °F.

2. Mix together cornmeal, flour, sugar, and baking powder.

3. In another bowl, combine buttermilk and egg. Beat lightly.

4. Slowly add buttermilk and egg mixture to dry ingredients.

5. Add margarine, and mix by hand or with mixer for 1 minute.

6. Bake for 20–25 minutes in an 8- by 8-inch, greased baking dish. Cool. Cut into 10 squares.

Yield: 10 servings
Serving size: 1 square
Each serving provides:
Calories: 178
Total fat: 6 g
Saturated fat: 1 g
Cholesterol: 22 mg
Sodium: 94 mg
Total fiber: 1 g
Protein: 4 g
Carbohydrates: 27 g
Potassium: 132 mg

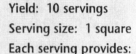

Homestyle Biscuits

Update your homestyle biscuits with this easy lowfat recipe.

2 C	flour
2 tsp	baking powder
$1/4$ tsp	baking soda
$1/4$ tsp	salt
2 Tbsp	sugar
$2/3$ C	1% fat buttermilk
$3^1/3$ Tbsp	vegetable oil

1. Preheat oven to 450 °F.

2. In medium bowl, combine flour, baking powder, baking soda, salt, and sugar.

3. In small bowl, stir together buttermilk and all of the oil. Pour over flour mixture and stir until well mixed.

4. On lightly floured surface, knead dough gently for 10–12 strokes. Roll or pat dough to $3/4$-inch thickness. Cut with 2-inch biscuit or cookie cutter, dipping cutter in flour between cuts. Transfer biscuits to an ungreased baking sheet.

5. Bake for 12 minutes or until golden brown. Serve warm.

Yield: 15 servings
Serving Size: 1, 2-inch biscuit
Each serving provides:
Calories: 99
Total fat: 3 g
Saturated fat: less than 1 g
Cholesterol: less than 1 mg
Sodium: 72 mg
Total fiber: 1 g
Protein: 2 g
Carbohydrates: 15 g
Potassium: 102 mg

Apple Coffee Cake

Apples and raisins keep this cake moist—which means less oil and more health.

5 C	tart apples, cored, peeled, chopped
1 C	sugar
1 C	dark raisins
1/2 C	pecans, chopped
1/4 C	vegetable oil
2 tsp	vanilla
1	egg, beaten
2 C	all-purpose flour, sifted
1 tsp	baking soda
2 tsp	ground cinnamon

1. Preheat oven to 350 °F.

2. Lightly oil 13- by 9- by 2-inch pan.

3. In large mixing bowl, combine apples with sugar, raisins, and pecans. Mix well and let stand for 30 minutes.

4. Stir in oil, vanilla, and egg. Sift together flour, soda, and cinnamon, and stir into apple mixture about a third at a time—just enough to moisten dry ingredients.

5. Turn batter into pan. Bake for 35–40 minutes. Cool cake slightly before serving.

Yield: 20 servings
Serving size: 1, 3 1/2-inch by 2 1/2-inch piece
Each serving provides:
Calories: 196
Total fat: 8 g
Saturated fat: 1 g
Cholesterol: 11 mg
Sodium: 67 mg
Total fiber: 2 g
Protein: 3 g
Carbohydrates: 31 g
Potassium: 136 mg

Frosted Cake

Use skim milk and lowfat cream cheese—and you can bake your cake and eat it too.

FOR CAKE

$2^1/4$ C	cake flour
$2^1/4$ tsp	baking powder
4 Tbsp	margarine
$1^1/4$ C	sugar
4	eggs
1 tsp	vanilla
1 Tbsp	orange peel
$3/4$ C	skim milk

FOR ICING

3 oz	lowfat cream cheese
2 Tbsp	skim milk
6 Tbsp	cocoa
2 C	confectioners' sugar, sifted
$1/2$ tsp	vanilla extract

Yield: 16 servings
Serving size: 1 slice
Each serving provides:
Calories: 241
Total fat: 5 g
Saturated fat: 2 g
Cholesterol: 57 mg
Sodium: 273 mg
Total fiber: 1 g
Protein: 4 g
Carbohydrates: 45 g
Potassium: 95 mg

To prepare cake:

1. Preheat oven to 325 °F.

2. Grease 10-inch round pan (at least 2 1/2 inches high) with small amount of cooking oil or use nonstick cooking oil spray. Powder pan with flour. Tap out excess flour.

3. Sift together flour and baking powder.

4. In separate bowl, beat together margarine and sugar until soft and creamy.

5. Beat in eggs, vanilla, and orange peel.

6. Gradually add flour mixture, alternating with milk, beginning and ending with flour.

continued on next page

Frosted Cake *(continued)*

7. Pour mixture into pan. Bake for 40–45 minutes or until done. Let cake cool for 5–10 minutes before removing from pan. Let cool completely before icing.

To prepare icing:

1. Cream together cream cheese and milk until smooth. Add cocoa. Blend well.

2. Slowly add sugar until icing is smooth. Mix in vanilla.

3. Smooth icing over top and sides of cooled cake.

Rainbow Fruit Salad

You can't go wrong
with this salad—
it's juicy, fresh,
naturally low in fat
and sodium, and
cholesterol free.
Enjoy it as a salad
or a dessert.

FOR FRUIT SALAD

1	large mango, peeled, diced
2 C	fresh blueberries
2	bananas, sliced
2 C	fresh strawberries, halved
2 C	seedless grapes
2	nectarines, unpeeled, sliced
1	kiwi fruit, peeled, sliced

FOR HONEY–ORANGE SAUCE

$1/3$ C	unsweetened orange juice
2 Tbsp	lemon juice
1 $1/2$ Tbsp	honey
$1/4$ tsp	ground ginger
dash	nutmeg

1. Prepare the fruit.
2. Combine all ingredients for sauce and mix.
3. Just before serving, pour honey–orange sauce over fruit.

Yield: 12 servings
Serving Size: 4-oz cup
Each serving provides:
Calories: 96
Total fat: 1 g
Saturated fat: less than 1 g
Cholesterol: 0 mg
Sodium: 4 mg
Total fiber: 3 g
Protein: 1 g
Carbohydrates: 24 g
Potassium: 302 mg

Tropical Fruit Compote

Fresh or cooked, fruits are a great low-calorie dessert.

3/4 C	water
1/2 C	sugar
2 tsp	fresh lemon juice
1 piece	lemon peel
1/2 tsp	rum or vanilla extract (optional)
1	pineapple, cored, peeled, cut into 8 slices
2	mangos, peeled, pitted, cut into 8 pieces
3	bananas, peeled, cut into 8 diagonal pieces
to taste	fresh mint leaves (optional)

► SERVING TIP

Top with lowfat or fat free sour cream.

1. In saucepan, combine 3/4 cup of water with sugar, lemon juice, and lemon peel (and rum or vanilla extract, if desired). Bring to boil, then reduce heat and add fruit. Cook at very low heat for 5 minutes.

2. Pour off syrup into cup.

3. Remove lemon rind from saucepan, and cool cooked fruit for 2 hours.

4. To serve, arrange fruit in serving dish and pour a few teaspoons of

Yield: 8 servings
Serving size: 1 cup
Each serving provides:
Calories: 148
Total fat: less than 1 g
Saturated fat: less than 1 g
Cholesterol: 0 mg
Sodium: 3 mg
Total fiber: 3 g
Protein: 1 g
Carbohydrates: 38 g
Potassium: 310 mg

Banana Mousse

This creamy dessert is a dream—yet low in saturated fat, cholesterol, and sodium.

2 Tbsp	lowfat milk
4 tsp	sugar
1 tsp	vanilla
1	medium banana, cut in quarters
1 C	plain lowfat yogurt
8 slices	(^{1}/4 inch each) banana

1. Place milk, sugar, vanilla, and banana in blender. Process for 15 seconds at high speed until smooth.

2. Pour mixture into small bowl and fold in yogurt. Chill.

3. Spoon into four dessert dishes and garnish each with two banana slices just before serving.

Yield: 4 servings
Serving size: ^{1}/2 cup
Each serving provides:
Calories: 94
Total fat: 1 g
Saturated fat: 1 g
Cholesterol: 4 mg
Sodium: 47 mg
Total fiber: 1 g
Protein: 1 g
Carbohydrates: 18 g
Potassium: 297 mg

Crunchy Pumpkin Pie

With only a small amount of oil in the crust and skim milk in the filling, this delicious pie is a heart healthy treat.

FOR CRUST

1 C	quick cooking oats
1/4 C	whole wheat flour
1/4 C	ground almonds
2 Tbsp	brown sugar
1/4 tsp	salt
3 Tbsp	vegetable oil
1 Tbsp	water

FOR FILLING

1/4 C	brown sugar, packed
1/2 tsp	ground cinnamon
1/4 tsp	ground nutmeg
1/4 tsp	salt
1	egg, beaten
4 tsp	vanilla
1 C	canned pumpkin
2/3 C	evaporated skim milk

Yield: 9 servings
Serving size: 1/9 of 9-inch pie
Each serving provides:
Calories: 169
Total fat: 7 g
Saturated fat: 1 g
Cholesterol: 24 mg
Sodium: 207 mg
Total fiber: 3 g
Protein: 5 g
Carbohydrates: 22 g
Potassium: 223 mg

1. Preheat oven to 425 °F.

To prepare crust:

2. Mix oats, flour, almonds, sugar, and salt in small mixing bowl.

3. Blend oil and water in measuring cup with fork or small wire whisk until emulsified.

4. Add oil mixture to dry ingredients and mix well. If needed, add small amount of water to hold mixture together.

5. Press into 9-inch pie pan, and bake for 8–10 minutes, or until light brown.

6. Turn down oven to 350 °F.

To prepare filling:

7. Mix sugar, cinnamon, nutmeg, and salt in bowl.

8. Add egg and vanilla, and mix to blend ingredients.

9. Add pumpkin and milk, and stir to combine.

Putting it together:

10. Pour filling into prepared pie shell.

11. Bake for 45 minutes at 350 °F or until knife inserted near center comes out clean.

Mock-Southern Sweet Potato Pie

There's nothing fake about the flavor in this heart healthy treat.

FOR CRUST

1¹/₄ C	flour
¹/₄ tsp	sugar
¹/₃ C	skim milk
2 Tbsp	vegetable oil

FOR FILLING

¹/₄ C	white sugar
¹/₄ C	brown sugar
¹/₂ tsp	salt
¹/₄ tsp	nutmeg
3	large eggs, beaten
¹/₄ C	canned evaporated skim milk
1 tsp	vanilla extract
3 C	sweet potatoes, cooked, mashed

Yield: 16 servings
Serving size: 1 slice
Each serving provides:
Calories: 147
Total fat: 3 g
Saturated fat: 1 g
Cholesterol: 40 mg
Sodium: 98 mg
Total fiber: 2 g
Protein: 4 g
Carbohydrates: 27 g
Potassium: 293 mg

1. Preheat oven to 350 °F.

To prepare crust:

2. Combine flour and sugar in bowl.

3. Add milk and oil to flour mixture.

4. Stir with fork until well mixed. Then form pastry into smooth ball with your hands.

5. Roll ball between two, 12-inch squares of waxed paper, using short, brisk strokes, until pastry reaches edge of paper.

6. Peel off top paper and invert crust into 9-inch pie plate.

To prepare filling:

7. Combine sugars, salt, nutmeg, and eggs.

8. Add milk and vanilla. Stir.

9. Add sweet potatoes and mix well.

Putting it together:

10. Pour mixture into pie shell.

11. Bake for 60 minutes or until crust is golden brown. Cool and cut into 16 slices.

Old-Fashioned Bread Pudding With Apple-Raisin Sauce

This old fashioned treat has been updated with a healthy spin. The sweet but healthy apple-raisin sauce makes a perfect topping—try it on fruit too.

FOR BREAD PUDDING

10 slices	whole wheat bread
3	egg whites
1 1/2 C	skim milk
1/4 C	white sugar
2 tsp	white sugar
1/4 C	brown sugar
1 tsp	vanilla extract
1/2 tsp	cinnamon
1/4 tsp	nutmeg
1/4 tsp	clove
as needed	vegetable oil spray

FOR APPLE-RAISIN SAUCE

1 1/4 C	apple juice
1/2 C	apple butter
2 Tbsp	molasses
1/2 C	raisins
1/4 tsp	ground cinnamon
1/4 tsp	ground nutmeg
1/2 tsp	orange zest (optional)

Yield for bread pudding: 9 servings
Yield for apple-raisin sauce: 2 cups
Serving size: 1/2 cup
Each serving (with apple-raisin sauce) provides:
Calories: 233
Total fat: 3 g
Saturated fat: 1 g
Cholesterol: 24 mg
Sodium: 252 mg
Total fiber: 3 g
Protein: 7 g
Carbohydrates: 46 g
Potassium: 390 mg

To prepare bread pudding:

1. Preheat oven to 350 °F.

2. Spray 8- by 8-inch baking dish with vegetable oil spray. Lay slices of bread in baking dish in two rows, overlapping like shingles.

3. In medium bowl, beat together egg, egg whites, milk, the 1/4 cup of white sugar, brown sugar, and vanilla. Pour egg mixture over bread.

4. In small bowl, stir together cinnamon, nutmeg, clove, and the 2 teaspoons of white sugar.

5. Sprinkle spiced sugar mix over bread pudding. Bake pudding for 30–35 minutes, until it has browned on top and is firm to touch. Serve warm or at room temperature with warm apple-raisin sauce.

To prepare apple-raisin sauce:

1. Stir all ingredients together in medium saucepan.

2. Bring to simmer over low heat. Let simmer for 5 minutes. Serve warm.

1-2-3 Peach Cobbler

What could be better than peach cobbler straight from the oven? Try this healthier version of the classic favorite.

1/2 tsp	ground cinnamon
1 Tbsp	vanilla extract
2 Tbsp	cornstarch
1 C	peach nectar
1/4 C	pineapple juice or peach juice (if desired, use juice reserved from canned peaches)
2 can	(16 oz each) peaches, packed in juice, drained, (or 1 3/4 lb fresh) sliced
1 Tbsp	tub margarine
1 C	dry pancake mix
2/3 C	all-purpose flour
1/2 C	sugar
2/3 C	evaporated skim milk
as needed	nonstick cooking spray
1/2 tsp	nutmeg
1 Tbsp	brown sugar

Yield: 8 servings
Serving size: 1 piece
Each serving provides:
Calories: 271
Total fat: 4 g
Saturated fat: less than 1 g
Cholesterol: less than 1 mg
Sodium: 263 mg
Total fiber: 2 g
Protein: 4 g
Carbohydrates: 54 g
Potassium: 284 mg

1. Combine cinnamon, vanilla, cornstarch, peach nectar, and pineapple or peach juice in saucepan over medium heat. Stir constantly until mixture thickens and bubbles.

2. Add sliced peaches to mixture.

3. Reduce heat and simmer for 5–10 minutes.

4. In another saucepan, melt margarine and set aside.

5. Lightly spray 8-inch-square glass dish with cooking spray. Pour hot peach mixture into dish.

6. In another bowl, combine pancake mix, flour, sugar, and melted margarine. Stir in milk. Quickly spoon this over peach mixture.

7. Combine nutmeg and brown sugar. Sprinkle on top of batter.

8. Bake at 400 °F for 15–20 minutes or until golden brown.

9. Cool and cut into 8 pieces.

Rice Pudding

Skim milk gives a whole lot of flavor without whole milk's fat and calories.

6 C	water
2 sticks	cinnamon
1 C	rice
3 C	skim milk
2/3 C	sugar
1/2 tsp	salt

1. Put water and cinnamon sticks into medium saucepan. Bring to boil.

2. Stir in rice. Cook on low heat for 30 minutes until rice is soft and water has evaporated.

3. Add skim milk, sugar, and salt. Cook for another 15 minutes until mixture thickens.

Yield: 5 servings
Serving size: 1/2 **cup**
Each serving provides:
Calories: 372
Total fat: 1 g
Saturated fat: less than 1 g
Cholesterol: 3 mg
Sodium: 366 mg
Total fiber: 1 g
Protein: 10 g
Carbohydrates: 81 g
Potassium: 363 mg

Winter Crisp

Only 1 tablespoon of margarine is used to make the crumb topping of this cholesterol-free, tart and tangy dessert.

FOR FILLING

1/2 C	sugar
3 Tbsp	all-purpose flour
1 tsp	lemon peel, grated
3/4 tsp	lemon juice
5 C	apples, unpeeled, sliced
1 C	cranberries

FOR TOPPING

2/3 C	rolled oats
1/3 C	brown sugar, packed
1/4 C	whole wheat flour
2 tsp	ground cinnamon
1 Tbsp	soft margarine, melted

Yield: 6 servings
Serving size: 1, 3/4-inch by 2-inch piece
Each serving provides (for Winter Crisp):
Calories: 252
Total fat: 2 g
Saturated fat: less than 1 g
Cholesterol: 0 mg
Sodium: 29 mg
Total fiber: 5 g
Protein: 3 g
Carbohydrates: 58 g
Potassium: 221 mg

1. Prepare filling by combining sugar, flour, and lemon peel in medium bowl. Mix well. Add lemon juice, apples, and cranberries. Stir to mix. Spoon into 6-cup baking dish.

2. Prepare topping by combining oats, brown sugar, flour, and cinnamon in small bowl. Add melted margarine. Stir to mix.

3. Sprinkle topping over filling. Bake in 375 °F oven for approximately 40–50 minutes or until filling is bubbly and top is brown. Serve warm or at room temperature.

Variation–Summer Crisp

Prepare as directed above, but substitute 4 cups fresh or unsweetened frozen peaches and 3 cups fresh or unsweetened frozen blueberries for apples and cranberries. If using frozen fruit, thaw peaches completely (use without draining), but do not thaw blueberries before adding to mixture.

Toppings AND Salad Dressings

Chili and Spice Seasoning

This spicy seasoning will heat up your catfish stew—and other dishes too.

1/4 C	paprika
2 Tbsp	dried oregano, crushed
2 tsp	chili powder
1 tsp	garlic powder
1 tsp	black pepper
1/2 tsp	red (cayenne) pepper
1/2 tsp	dry mustard

Mix together all ingredients. Store in airtight container.

Yield: 1/3 cup
Serving size: 1 tablespoon
Each serving provides:
Calories: 26
Total fat: 1 g
Saturated fat: 0 g
Cholesterol: 0 mg
Sodium: 13 mg
Total fiber: 2 g
Protein: 1 g
Carbohydrates: 5 g
Potassium: 180 mg

Fresh Salsa

Fresh herbs add plenty of flavor to this salsa—so you use less salt.

6	tomatoes, preferably Roma (or 3 large tomatoes)
$1/2$	medium onion, finely chopped
1 clove	garlic, finely minced
2	jalapeño peppers, finely chopped
3 Tbsp	cilantro, chopped
to taste	fresh lime juice
$1/8$ tsp	oregano, finely crushed
$1/8$ tsp	salt
$1/8$ tsp	pepper
$1/2$	avocado, diced (black skin)

1. Combine all ingredients in glass bowl.

2. Serve immediately or refrigerate and serve within 4–5 hours.

Yield: 8 servings
Serving size: $1/2$ cup
Each serving provides:
Calories: 42
Total fat: 2 g
Saturated fat: less than 1 g
Cholesterol: 0 mg
Sodium: 44 mg
Total fiber: 2 g
Protein: 1 g
Carbohydrates: 7 g
Potassium : 337 mg

Hot 'N Spicy Seasoning

1^1/$_2$ tsp	white pepper
^{1}/$_2$ tsp	cayenne pepper
^{1}/$_2$ tsp	black pepper
1 tsp	onion powder
1^1/$_4$ tsp	garlic powder
1 Tbsp	basil, dried
1^1/$_2$ tsp	thyme, dried

Spices can make the ordinary extraordinary. Here's a great all-purpose spice mix.

▶SERVING TIP

Try this mix with meat, poultry, fish, or vegetable dishes. Use it instead of salt—even in the salt shaker.

Mix all ingredients together. Store in an airtight container.

Yield: ^{1}/$_3$ cup
Serving Size: ^{1}/$_2$ teaspoon
Each serving provides:
Calories: 1
Total fat: 1 g
Saturated fat: 0 g
Cholesterol: 0 mg
Sodium: 0 mg
Total fiber: 0 g
Protein: 0 g
Carbohydrates: less than 1 g
Potassium: 4 mg

Vinaigrette Salad Dressing

Try this recipe to dress up a salad for a special meal.

1 bulb	garlic, separated into cloves, peeled
1/2 C	water
1 Tbsp	red wine vinegar
1/4 tsp	honey
1 Tbsp	virgin olive oil
1/2 tsp	black pepper

1. Place garlic cloves into small saucepan and pour in enough water (about 1/2 cup) to cover them.

2. Bring water to boil, then reduce heat and simmer until garlic is tender (about 15 minutes).

3. Reduce liquid to 2 tablespoons and increase heat for 3 minutes.

4. Pour contents into small sieve over bowl. With wooden spoon, mash garlic through sieve.

5. Whisk vinegar into garlic mixture, then mix in oil and seasoning.

Yield: 4 servings
Serving size:
2 tablespoons
Each serving provides:
Calories: 33
Total fat: 3 g
Saturated fat: 1 g
Cholesterol: 0 mg
Sodium: 0 mg
Total fiber: 0 g
Protein: 0 g
Carbohydrates: 1 g
Potassium: 9 mg

Yogurt Salad Dressing

So easy—
so healthy—
so good.
Try it!

8 oz	fat free plain yogurt
$1/4$ C	fat free mayonnaise
2 Tbsp	chives, dried
2 Tbsp	dill, dried
2 Tbsp	lemon juice

Mix all ingredients in bowl and refrigerate.

Yield: 8 servings
Serving size:
2 tablespoons
Each serving provides:
Calories: 23
Total fat: 0 g
Saturated fat: 0 g
Cholesterol: 1 mg
Total fiber: 0 g
Sodium: 84 mg
Protein: 2 g
Carbohydrates: 4 g
Potassium: 104 mg

BEVERAGES

Mango Shake

Kids love this drink's creamy, sweet taste.

2 C	lowfat milk
4 Tbsp	frozen mango juice (or 1 fresh mango, pitted)
1	small banana
2	ice cubes

Put all ingredients into blender. Blend until foamy. Serve immediately.

Variations

Instead of mango juice, try orange, papaya, or strawberry juice.

Yield: 4 servings

Serving size: $3/4$ **cup**

Each serving provides (with mango and banana):

Calories: 106

Total fat: 2 g

Saturated fat: 1 g

Cholesterol: 5 mg

Sodium: 63 mg

Total fiber: 2 g

Protein: 5 g

Carbohydrates: 20 g

Potassium: 361 mg

Summer Breezes Smoothie

Here's a perfect lowfat thirst quencher.

1 C	fat free, plain yogurt
6	medium strawberries
1 C	pineapple, crushed, canned in juice
1	medium banana
1 tsp	vanilla extract
4	ice cubes

1. Place all ingredients in blender and puree until smooth.
2. Serve in frosted glass.

Yield: 3 servings
Serving size: 1 cup
Each serving provides:
Calories: 121
Total fat: less than 1 g
Saturated fat: less than 1 g
Cholesterol: 1 mg
Sodium: 64 mg
Total fiber: 2 g
Protein: 6 g
Carbohydrates: 24 g
Potassium: 483 mg

CPSIA information can be obtained
at www.ICGtesting.com
Printed in the USA
LVOW12s1039010717

540042LV00001B/86/P